OUR MANY SELVES

D0168775

OUR MANY SELVES

PRACTICAL YOGIC PSYCHOLOGY

Selections from the Works of
SRI AUROBINDO
and
THE MOTHER

Compiled with an Introduction by
A. S. Dalal

LOTUS PRESS
P O Box 325
Twin Lakes, WI 53181 USA

This book was first published by Sri Aurobindo Ashram Publication Department, Pondicherry, India, in 2002.

First Lotus Press edition 2002

Published by:
LOTUS PRESS
P O Box 325
Twin Lakes, WI 53181 USA
262 889 8561
email: lotuspress@lotuspress.com
website: www.lotuspress.com

ISBN 0-940985-34-9

Library of Congress Control Number 2002106366

Printed at Sri Aurobindo Ashram Press, Pondicherry
PRINTED IN INDIA

CONTENTS

Contents

Contents

Contents

... as Being is one yet multiple, so also the same law prevails in ourselves and our members; the Spirit, the Purusha is one but it adapts itself to the formations of Nature. Over each grade of our being a power of the Spirit presides; we have within us and discover when we go deep enough inwards a mind-self, a life-self, a physical self; there is a being of mind, a mental Purusha, expressing something of itself on our surface in the thoughts, perceptions, activities of our mind-nature, a being of life which expresses something of itself in the impulses, feelings, sensations, desires, external life-activities of our vital nature, a physical being, a being of the body which expresses something of itself in the instincts, habits, formulated activities of our physical nature. These beings or part selves of the self in us are powers of the Spirit and therefore not limited by their temporary expression, for what is thus formulated is only a fragment of its possibilities; but the expression creates a temporary mental, vital or physical personality which grows and develops even as the psychic being or soul-personality grows and develops within us. Each has its own distinct nature, its influence, its action on the whole of us; but on our surface all these influences and all this action, as they come up, mingle and create an aggregate surface being which is a composite, an amalgam of them all, an outer persistent and yet shifting and mobile formation for the purposes of this life and its limited experience.

Sri Aurobindo

(*The Life Divine*, SABCL, Vol. 19, pp. 896-97)

If you have the philosophic mind, you will ask yourself: "What do I call 'myself'? Is it my body? — it changes all the time, it is never the same thing. Is it my feelings? — they change so often. Is it my thoughts? — they are built and destroyed continuously. That is not myself. Where is the self? What is it that gives me this sense of continuity?" If you continue sincerely, you go back a few years. The problem becomes more and more perplexing. You continue to observe, you tell yourself: "It is my memory." But even if one loses one's memory, one would be oneself. If one sincerely continues this profound search, there comes a moment when everything disappears and one single thing exists, that is the Divine, the divine Presence. Everything disappears, dissolves, everything melts away like butter in the sunlight.... When one has made this discovery, one becomes aware that one was nothing but a bundle of habits. It is always that which does not know the Divine and is not conscious of the Divine which speaks. In everyone there are these hundreds and hundreds of "selves" who speak and in hundreds of completely different ways — "selves" unconscious, changing, fluid. The self which speaks today is not the same as yesterday's; and if you look further, the self has disappeared. There is only one who remains. That is the Divine. It is the only one that may be seen always the same.

The Mother

(*Questions and Answers 1953*, CWM, Vol. 5, p. 17)

PREFACE

Yoga is generally associated with certain set practices such as postures, breathing exercises, meditation and the like. In addition, yoga is understood as consisting in certain rules and norms pertaining to aspects of one's outer life, such as diet, habits and acts of conduct. However, as taught by Sri Aurobindo, yoga consists essentially in inner psychological work aimed at the change and transformation of consciousness. As he states: "Yoga is nothing but practical psychology"[1]; "...the whole method of Yoga is psychological; it might almost be termed the consummate practice of a perfect psychological knowledge."[2]

This book, meant primarily for the general spiritual seeker rather than for the practitioner of Sri Aurobindo's Integral Yoga, deals only with the initial and preliminary steps towards the radical change of consciousness aimed at by the Integral Yoga. These initial tasks of psychospiritual growth consist in: emerging progressively from the unconscious state in which one is more or less a fused part of the collective mass rather than an independent individual who is "a truly mental man who thinks for himself, is free from all outer influences, who has an individuality, who exists, has his reality" (p. 104); developing an increasingly greater understanding of oneself by becoming more and more conscious of one's being in all its complexity in order to discern the springs of

1. Sri Aurobindo, *The Synthesis of Yoga*, Sri Aurobindo Birth Centenary Library, Vol. 20, p. 39.
2. *Ibid.*, p. 496.

one's actions arising from the different parts of one's being so as to be able to exercise self-control and attain self-mastery; bringing harmony and order among the diverse parts of one's being which normally are in a state of conflict and disorder; discovering one's true self and unifying one's being — which is normally characterised by division and disunity — by organising all other selves around the true self.

The reader may notice that the majority of passages in this book have been drawn from the works of the Mother because her works consist mostly of the talks she gave to the young folk of the Ashram school to whom she taught in practical terms the preliminary work of inner growth just mentioned above.

Self-understanding is the first step. As the Mother remarks:

"First learn to know yourself perfectly and then to control yourself perfectly."[3]

"To perfect oneself, one must first become conscious of oneself."[4]

"The distinct character of man", states Sri Aurobindo, "is that he is a mental being".[5] Therefore man naturally starts with a mental understanding of himself. A mental self-understanding lies in being able to distinguish intellectually the

3. The Mother, *Words of the Mother*, Collected Works of the Mother, Vol. 14, p. 272.

4. The Mother, *Questions and Answers 1950-51*, Collected Works of the Mother, Vol. 4, p. 34.

5. Sri Aurobindo, *The Synthesis of Yoga*, Sri Aurobindo Birth Centenary Library, Vol. 20, p. 73.

many different and complex parts of one's being. This calls for "a very long training and a long discipline of study and observation",[6] to identify the respective sources of one's thoughts, feelings, actions and moods. This means being able to give a "label" to the different parts of our make-up which constitute the many selves of our being. To many people "label" and "labelling" have a somewhat pejorative meaning, being associated with a mere mental or intellectual process, devoid of a true understanding of the thing being labelled, and often acting as an obstacle to a true understanding. However, a mental understanding is not necessarily an obstacle. On the contrary, it can be a great aid and a step towards deeper understanding. To shun all mental or intellectual understanding as mere "labelling" is to ignore the fact, stated above, that the distinct character of the human being is that of a mental being, and it is but natural for one to start with a mental understanding and gradually develop a deeper understanding. It is only rare individuals who have a deep self-understanding so as to be able to distinguish the different inner movements of their many selves without having first learnt to label them mentally. As the Mother once said to the children of the Ashram school:

"...if nobody has ever taught you what the psychic or the vital is, you cannot have any notion of the thing. You may say, 'Today I feel good, yesterday I did not.' Till I was twenty-four I knew nothing about all these things, and yet I could distinguish very well these movements. I did not

6. The Mother, *Questions and Answers 1957-58*, Collected Works of the Mother, Vol. 9, p. 308.

use these words because no one had taught them to me and I had never read anything, but I felt very clearly the difference at different moments and in what state of consciousness I was.

"But you who are here, after all that you have heard and all that you have read and all that I have taught you, you should be conversant with all the movements within you and be able to fix a little label: this is this, that is this other."[7]

Sri Aurobindo states that it is necessary to distinguish clearly the different parts of one's being not only for the sake of intellectual clarity but also for avoiding confusion in one's experience in sadhana.[8] Thus, for example, with regard to the distinction between the individual self (Jivatman) — which constitutes a single centre of the multiple Divine — and the all-embracing Divine itself, Sri Aurobindo remarks: "It is important to remember the distinction; for, otherwise, if there is the least vital egoism, one may begin to think of oneself as an Avatar...."[9]

Another example of confusion caused by the inability to distinguish between different parts of the being pertains to the distinction between the psychic being or soul and parts of the being (mental and emotional) which are merely under the influence of the psychic being but are often mistaken to

7. The Mother, *Questions and Answers 1954*, Collected Works of the Mother, Vol. 6, p. 7.

8. Sri Aurobindo, *Letters on Yoga*, Sri Aurobindo Birth Centenary Library, Vol. 22, p. 276.

9. *Ibid.*, p. 266.

be the psychic being itself (pp. 91-93).

Regarding the importance of such a discrimination, Sri Aurobindo writes:

"There is the true psychic which is always good and there is the psychic opening to mental, vital and other worlds which contain all kinds of things good, bad and indifferent, true, false and half true, thought-suggestions which are of all kinds, and messages also which are of all kinds. What is needed is not to give yourself impartially to all of them but to develop both a sufficient knowledge and experience and a sufficient discrimination to be able to keep your balance and eliminate falsehood, half-truths and mixtures. It will not do to dismiss impatiently the necessity for discrimination on the ground that that is mere intellectualism. The discrimination need not be intellectual, although that also is a thing not to be despised."[10]

Thus even a purely intellectual discrimination, not yet founded on experience, is valuable and "a thing not to be despised".

A crucial distinction that one needs to make on the spiritual path is the difference between the psychical and the spiritual. Due to an inadequate knowledge of yogic psychology, psychical phenomena and experiences — which pertain to the *inner* or subliminal consciousness, a realm of darkness as well as light — are often confused with spiritual experiences, which pertain to the *higher* consciousness.

---

10. Sri Aurobindo, *Letters on Yoga*, Sri Aurobindo Birth Centenary Library, Vol. 23, p. 1047.

Regarding the vague and imprecise way in which the term "spiritual" is used not only in popular literature but also in serious writings, the Mother remarks:

> "... philosophical, yogic and other systems use the word 'spiritual' in a very vague and loose way. Whatever is not physical is spiritual! In comparison with the physical world all other worlds are spiritual! All thought, all effort which does not tend towards the material life is a spiritual effort. Every tendency which is not strictly human and egoistic is a spiritual tendency. This is a word used to season every dish."[11]

The distinction between the inner or supraphysical consciousness and the higher or spiritual consciousness is one of the most valuable aspects of yogic psychology for promoting the self-understanding of the spiritual seeker.

Self-understanding must lead to self-mastery. As the Mother, explaining the meaning of her phrase, "to know oneself and control oneself", says:

> "This means to be conscious of one's inner truth, conscious of the different parts of one's being and their respective functions. You must know why you do this, why you do that; you must know your thoughts, know your feelings, all your activities, all your movements, of what you are capable, etc. And to know oneself is not enough:

11. The Mother, *Questions and Answers 1950-51*, Collected Works of the Mother, Vol. 4, p. 226.

this knowledge must bring a conscious control. To know oneself perfectly is to control oneself perfectly."[12]

These statements imply that an understanding of the different parts of one's being constituting our different selves must result in self-control and self-mastery if the mental understanding is to become true self-knowledge. But true self-mastery can come about only when the different parts of the being — which are normally divided and conflicted — are unified around the inmost centre of our being, the soul or psychic being. As the Mother remarks, "This unification is indispensable if one wants to be the master of one's being and of all its actions."[13]

Traditionally, the term "yoga" — which literally means "union" — has been generally understood as a path which aims at achieving the union of the individual self with the Universal Self so as to lead to liberation from the ignorance and suffering of life on earth. In Sri Aurobindo's yoga, which aims at not only the liberation of the individual soul but also the transformation of earthly life, yoga implies not only union of the individual soul with the Divine but also the union of the outer being with the soul and the unification of one's being around the soul, for, according to Sri Aurobindo and the Mother, it is only through such a unification of one's being that the Divine can be made to manifest and transform the earthly life.

A. S. D.

12. *Ibid.,* p. 34.
13. The Mother, *Some Answers from the Mother*, Collected Works of the Mother, Vol. 16, p. 396.

INTRODUCTION

SRI AUROBINDO ON OUR MANY SELVES:
PLANES AND PARTS OF THE BEING

"Man is in his self a unique Person, but he is also in his manifestation of self a multiperson..."[1] In this statement Sri Aurobindo makes a distinction which is fundamental in understanding his explanation of the nature of the human being — the distinction between the Person and its many personalities. This distinction is far from apparent to us in our ordinary consciousness.

> "The ordinary mind knows itself only as an ego with all the movements of the nature in a jumble and, identifying itself with these movements, thinks 'I am doing this, feeling that, thinking, in joy or in sorrow etc.' The first beginning of real self-knowledge is when you feel yourself separate from the nature in you and its movements and then you see that there are many parts of your being, many personalities each acting on its own behalf and in its own way."[2]

We do not possess self-knowledge because we know ourselves not as the Person but as an ego, which is an identification of the Person with the many personalities that constitute the outer nature of our being. In terms of Sankhya philosophy, we do not know ourselves as the Purusha (Person) because we are identified with Prakriti (Nature). In this state of identification with Prakriti, the complex nature of our being is hidden from our view.

"To the ordinary man who lives upon his own waking surface, ignorant of the self's depths and vastnesses behind the veil, his psychological existence is fairly simple. A small but clamorous company of desires, some imperative intellectual and aesthetic cravings, some tastes, a few ruling or prominent ideas amid a great current of unconnected or ill-connected and mostly trivial thoughts, a number of more or less imperative vital needs, alternations of physical health and disease, a scattered and inconsequent succession of joys and griefs, frequent minor disturbances and vicissitudes and rarer strong searchings and upheavals of mind or body, and through it all Nature, partly with the aid of his thought and will, partly without or in spite of it, arranging these things in some rough practical fashion, some tolerable disorderly order, — this is the material of his existence."[3]

Real self-knowledge begins when a separation takes place between Purusha and Prakriti, between the Self and its outer Nature. We then perceive "the extraordinary complexity of our own being, the stimulating but also embarrassing multiplicity of our personality, the rich endless confusion of Nature."[4]

We also perceive that the numerous personalities, which are mixed up on the surface, are separate and distinct when viewed from within. Each personality represents a part of the being which has its own complex individuality and different nature, its own demands, agreeing neither with itself nor with the others. Speaking of the "perfectly normal divisibility of the different parts of the being", Sri Aurobindo states:

"In the outer surface nature, mind, psychic, vital, physical are all jumbled together and it needs a strong power of introspection, self-analysis, close observation and disentanglement of the threads of thought, feeling and impulse to find out the composition of our nature and the relation and interaction of these parts upon each other. But when one goes inside... we find the sources of all this surface action and there the parts of our being are quite separate and clearly distinct from each other. We feel them indeed as different beings in us, and just as two people in a joint action can do, they too are seen to observe, criticise, help or oppose and restrain each other; it is as if we were a group-being, each member of the group with its separate place and function, and all directed by a central being who is sometimes in front above the others, sometimes behind the scenes."[5]

Two Systems in the Organisation of the Being

From the viewpoint of Sri Aurobindo's thought, the human being is inseparably one with the universal being. There are, he says, "two systems simultaneously active in the organisation of the being and its parts"[6] — a concentric system and a vertical system.

The concentric system is like a series of rings or sheaths, consisting of the outer being, the inner being and the inmost being. The outer being and the inner being behind it constitute our phenomenal or instrumental being and are said to belong to Nature or Prakriti. They have three corresponding

parts — physical, vital, mental. The inmost being is the
Purusha, the true being. In the Purusha, there is an inmost
mental, an inmost vital and an inmost physical, and, at the
very core, the psychic being or soul. The psychic being is
usually referred to as the inmost being (Fig. 1).

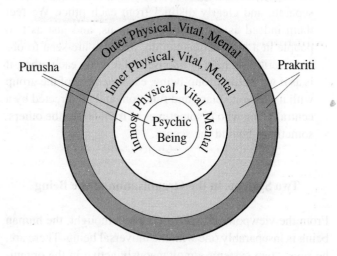

FIG. 1. THE CONCENTRIC SYSTEM

The vertical system is like a staircase, consisting of various levels, planes or gradations of consciousness ranging
from the lowest — the Inconscient — to the highest, Sachchidananda (Fig. 2).

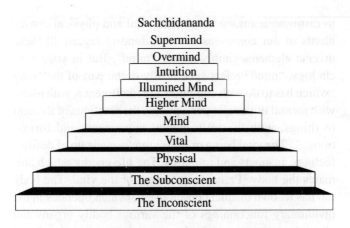

FIG.2. THE VERTICAL SYSTEM – LEVELS OF CONSCIOUSNESS

Note: Ancient Indian wisdom divided the human being, the microcosm, as well as the world-being, the macrocosm, into a higher hemisphere, Parardha, and a lower hemisphere, Apararadha. The higher hemisphere is where the Spirit reigns perfectly and eternally; in the lower hemisphere, the Spirit is veiled by mind, life and body. Overmind is the intermediary plane dividing the two hemispheres.

The main parts and planes of the being as described by Sri Aurobindo are explained below.

The Outer Being

There are three main parts in the outer or surface being: the mind (the mental), the life-nature (the vital) and the body (the physical). Each part has its own distinct type of consciousness, though in our ordinary awareness we are unable to distinguish among the mental, vital and physical constituents of our consciousness, and tend to regard all these diverse elements simply as our "mind". But in yoga psychology, "mind" refers specifically to the part of the being "which has to do with cognition and intelligence, with ideas, with mental or thought perceptions, the reactions of thought to things, with the truly mental movements and formations..."[7] The vital being or life-nature is made up of desires, feelings, instincts and impulses. The life-energy which animates the body (Prana) is an aspect of the vital. The body too has its own distinct consciousness which operates in the involuntary functionings of the various bodily organs and physiological systems. Body-consciousness is only part of the physical consciousness. The latter includes also the physical mind and the physical vital which will be presently explained.

Though separate and distinct, the three main divisions of the outer being just mentioned are interconnected and interact on one another, giving rise to distinguishable subdivisions in the main parts of the being. Thus besides the thinking mind (the mind proper), there is a vital mind, which is the part of the mind that is intermixed with the vital. The vital mind, unlike the thinking mind, is not governed by reason but is dominated by impulses and desires of the vital, and seeks to justify and rationalise actions which are based on impulses and desires of the vital. Another subdivision is the physical mind, which is the part of the mind that is intermixed with the physical, and partakes of the characteristics of the physical consciousness such as inertia, obscurity and mechanical repetitiveness which manifest in the physical mind as mental torpor and conservatism, doubt, and obsessive thoughts. The part of the mind which is closest to the physical is called the mechanical mind; its characteristic is that of a machine that goes on turning round and round whenever thoughts occur in it. Another subdivision which is important for self-understanding is the physical vital; it is the part of the vital which is turned entirely upon physical things, and is full of desires and seekings for pleasure on the physical plane. Closely connected with it is the vital physical, the part of the vital force which constitutes the nervous being; it is the vehicle of the nervous responses and is related to the reactions, desires and sensations of the body.

The Inner Being (The Subliminal)

Behind the surface or frontal consciousness of the outer being there is an inner or subliminal consciousness upon all the three levels — physical, vital, mental. Thus there is an inner mind, an inner vital and an inner physical. The inner mind is in touch with the universal mind, the inner vital with the universal life-forces, and the inner physical with the universal physical forces around us. Thus whereas the outer being knows things only indirectly from their outer touches as perceived though the senses and the outer mind, the inner being is directly aware of the surrounding universal forces that act through us.

Environmental Consciousness (*The Circumconscient*)

The inner or subliminal being receives the contacts of the

environing world though the environmental consciousness or the circumconscient, a formation of the subliminal consciousness which projects itself beyond the body.

"It is through this [environmental consciousness] that the thoughts, feelings etc. of others pass to enter into one — it is through this also that waves of the universal force — desire, sex, etc. come in and take possession of the mind, vital or body."[8]

"Each man has his own personal consciousness entrenched in his body and gets into touch with his surroundings only through his body and senses and the mind using the senses.

"Yet all the time the universal forces are pouring into him without his knowing it. He is aware only of thoughts, feelings, etc., that rise to the surface and these he takes for his own. Really they come from outside in mind waves, vital waves, waves of feeling and sensation, etc., which take particular form in him and rise to the surface after they have got inside.

"But they do not get into his body at once. He carries about with him an environmental consciousness (called by the Theosophists the Aura) into which they first enter. If you can become conscious of this environmental self of yours, then you can catch the thought, passion, suggestion or force of illness and prevent it from entering into you."[9]

The Inmost Being — The Psychic Being

Sri Aurobindo uses the term "psychic being" (from Greek *psukhē*, meaning the soul) for the inmost being which supports the outer and the inner beings. The psychic being in its essence, called the psyche or psychic entity, is a spark or portion of the Divine present in all things and creatures. In the course of evolution the psyche grows into an individual psychic personality in the human being and is then called the psychic being.

Whereas the universal Self, the Atman, is unborn, and stands above the evolutionary process and is unaffected by it, the psychic being is the evolving soul which, though immortal, passes through cycles of physical birth and death, growing from life to life.

> "The psychic being can at first exercise only a concealed and partial and indirect action through the mind, the life and the body, since it is these parts of Nature that have to be developed as its instruments of self-expression, and it is long confined by their evolution. Missioned to lead man in the Ignorance towards the light of the Divine Consciousness, it takes the essence of all experience in the Ignorance to form a nucleus of soul-growth in the nature; the rest it turns into material for the future growth of the instruments which it has to use until they are ready to be a luminous instrumentation of the Divine.... It is the psychic personality in us that flowers as the saint, the sage, the seer; when it reaches its full strength, it turns the being towards the Knowledge of Self and the Divine,

towards the supreme Truth, the supreme Good, the supreme Beauty, Love and Bliss, the divine heights and
largenesses, and opens us to the touch of spiritual sym-
pathy, universality, oneness."[10]

The Subconscient and the Inconscient

The subconscient is what is *below* the mind and conscious
life just as the subliminal is what is *behind* the outer consciousness. Whereas the subliminal is an inner and larger
consciousness compared to the surface consciousness, the
subconscious is a nether and inferior, diminished consciousness.

"[The subconscient] covers the purely physical and vital
elements of our constitution of bodily being, unmen-
talised, unobserved by the mind, uncontrolled by it in
their action. It can be held to include the dumb occult
consciousness, dynamic but not sensed by us, which operates in the cells and nerves and all the corporeal stuff
and adjusts their life process and automatic responses. It
covers also those lowest functionings of submerged
sense-mind which are more operative in the animal and
in plant life; in our evolution we have overpassed the need
of any large organised action of this element, but it remains submerged and obscurely at work below our conscious nature. This obscure activity extends to a hidden
and hooded mental substratum into which past impressions and all that is rejected from the surface mind sink

and remain there dormant and can surge up in sleep or in any absence of the mind, taking dream forms, forms of mechanical mind-action or suggestion, forms of automatic vital reaction or impulse, forms of physical abnormality or nervous perturbance, forms of morbidity, disease, unbalance. Out of the subconscious we bring ordinarily so much to the surface as our waking sense-mind and intelligence need for their purpose; in so bringing them up we are not aware of their nature, origin, operation and do not apprehend them in their own values but by a translation into the values of our waking human sense and intelligence. But the risings of the subconscious, its effects upon the mind and body, are mostly automatic, uncalled for and involuntary; for we have no knowledge and therefore no control of the subconscient."[11]

Below the subconscient is the Inconscient, the nethermost plane of consciousness. It is not really devoid of consciousness as the term might imply, but a level of consciousness which represents a total involution of consciousness, the "inverse reproduction of the supreme superconscience".[12] Evolution begins from the Inconscient, the first emergence to evolve from it being Matter.

The Superconscient

The superconscient consists of higher levels of consciousness above the ordinary mind from which the higher consciousness comes down into the lower planes of the being. "The role of the superconscient has been to evolve slowly the spiritual man out of the mental half-animal."[13] The superconscient includes the higher planes of mind — Higher Mind, Illumined Mind, Intuition and Overmind — as well as what is beyond mind, namely, Supermind and the Supreme Reality called Sachchidananda (Existence-Consciousness-Bliss). These superconscient gradations of consciousness are here briefly described in Sri Aurobindo's words.

Higher Mind

"I mean by the Higher Mind a first plane of spiritual consciousness where one becomes constantly and closely aware of the Self, the One everywhere and knows and sees things habitually with that awareness; but it is still very much on the mind level although highly spiritual in its essential substance; and its instrumentation is through an elevated thought-power and comprehensive mental sight — not illumined by any of the intenser upper lights but as if in a large strong and clear daylight. It acts as an intermediate state between the Truth-Light above and the human mind; communicating the higher knowledge in a form that the Mind intensified, broadened, made spiritually supple, can receive without being blinded or dazzled by a Truth beyond it."[14]

Illumined Mind

"...a Mind no longer of higher Thought, but of spiritual light. Here the clarity of the spiritual intelligence, its tranquil daylight, gives place or subordinates itself to an intense lustre, a splendour and illumination of the Spirit: a play of lightnings of spiritual truth and power breaks from above into the consciousness and adds to the calm and wide enlightenment and the vast descent of peace which characterise or accompany the action of the larger conceptual-spiritual principle, a fiery ardour of realisation and a rapturous ecstasy of knowledge."[15]

Intuition*

"Intuition is a power of consciousness nearer and more intimate to the original knowledge by identity; for it is always something that leaps out direct from a concealed identity. It is when the consciousness of the subject meets with the consciousness in the object, penetrates it and sees, feels or vibrates with the truth of what it contacts, that the intuition leaps out like a spark or lightning-flash from the shock of the meeting; or when the consciousness, even without any such meeting, looks into itself and feels directly and intimately the truth or the truths that are there or so contacts the hidden forces behind appearances, then also there is the outbreak of an intuitive light; or, again, when the consciousness meets the Supreme Reality or the spiritual reality of things and

---

* Ordinarily, intuition means the power of understanding things immediately, without the need for conscious reasoning. In this ordinary sense, intuition may be based on a feeling, or it may be a rapid "subconscious reasoning" based on subtle cues which are not consciously apprehended. But as employed by Sri Aurobindo to refer to the superconscient plane above the Illumined Mind, the term has a much deeper connotation.

beings and has a contactual union with it, then the spark, the flash or the blaze of intimate truth-perception is lit in its depths."[16]

Overmind

"...the overmind knows the One as the support, essence, fundamental power of all things, but in the dynamic play proper to it it lays emphasis on its divisional power of multiplicity and seeks to give each power or Aspect its full chance to manifest, relying on the underlying One-ness to prevent disharmony or conflict. Each Godhead, as it were, creates his own world, but without conflict with others; each Aspect, each Idea, each Force of things can be felt in its full separate energy or splendour and work out its values, but this does not create a disharmony, because the overmind has the sense of the Infinite and in the true (not spatial) Infinite many concording infinities are possible."[17]

"In its nature and law the Overmind is a delegate of the Supermind Consciousness, its delegate to the Ignorance. Or we might speak of it as a protective double, a screen of dissimilar similarity through which Supermind can act indirectly on an Ignorance whose darkness could not bear or receive the direct impact of a supreme Light. Even, it is by the projection of this luminous Overmind corona that the diffusion of a diminished light in the Ignorance and the throwing of that contrary shadow which swallows up in itself all light, the Inconscience, became at all possible. For Supermind transmits to Overmind all its realities, but leaves it to formulate them in a movement and according to an awareness of things which is still a vision of Truth and yet at the same time a first parent of the Ignorance."[18]

Supermind*

"The Supermind is in its very essence a truth-consciousness, a consciousness always free from the Ignorance which is the foundation of our present natural or evolutionary existence and from which nature in us is trying to arrive at self-knowledge and world-knowledge and a right consciousness and the right use of our existence in the universe. The Supermind, because it is a truth-consciousness, has this knowledge inherent in it and this power of true existence; its course is straight and can go direct to its aim, its field is wide and can even be made illimitable. This is because its very nature is knowledge: it has not to acquire knowledge but possesses it in its own right; its steps are not from nescience or ignorance into some imperfect light, but from truth to greater truth, from right perception to deeper perception, from intuition to intuition, from illumination to utter and boundless luminousness, from growing

* The term "Supermind" is apt to convey the sense of a super-eminent mind which is far above the ordinary mind. However Sri Aurobindo means by it a superconscient plane of being which is not only above the mind but also *beyond* mind and *radically different* from it. It is beyond and different not only in relation to the ordinary mind but also in comparison with the superconscient planes of mind, namely, Higher Mind, Illumined Mind, Intuition and Overmind. For whereas all these superconscient planes of mind are blends of light and darkness, Knowledge-Ignorance, Supermind is the Truth-Consciousness, totally devoid of Ignorance.

widenesses to the utter vasts and to very infinitude. On its summits it possesses the divine omniscience and omnipotence, but even in an evolutionary movement of its own graded self-manifestation by which it would eventually reveal its own highest heights it must be in its very nature essentially free from ignorance and error: it starts from truth and light and moves always in truth and light."[19]

Sachchidananda (*Existence-Consciousness-Bliss*)

"It [Sachchidananda] is one eternal Existence that we then are, one eternal Consciousness which sees its own works in us and others, one eternal Will or Force of that Consciousness which displays itself in infinite workings, one eternal Delight which has the joy of itself and all its workings, — itself stable, immutable, timeless, spaceless, supreme and itself still in the infinity of its workings, not changed by their variations, not broken up by their multiplicity, not increased or diminished by their ebbings and flowings in the seas of Time and Space, not confused by their apparent contrarieties or limited by their divinely-willed limitations. Sachchidananda is the unity of the many-sidedness of manifested things, the eternal harmony of all their variations and oppositions, the infinite perfection which justifies their limitations and is the goal of their imperfections."[20]

The traditional Path of Knowledge (Jnana Yoga) in India aims at eliminating successively the body, the life and the mind and taking a straight plunge by merging into the supracosmic Reality of Sachchidananda. However, for an integral self-knowledge, says Sri Aurobindo, it is necessary to ascend through each of the superconscient planes including the Supermind in the passage to Sachchidananda.

"The method of the traditional way of knowledge, eliminating all these things, [body, life, mind] arrives at the conception and realisation of a pure conscious existence, self-aware, self-blissful, unconditioned by mind and life and body and to its ultimate positive experience that is Atman, the Self, the original and essential nature of our existence. Here at last there is something centrally true, but in its haste to arrive at it this knowledge assumes that there is nothing between the thinking mind and the Highest, *buddheḥ paratastu saḥ*,* and, shutting its eyes in Samadhi, tries to rush through all that actually intervenes without even seeing these great and luminous kingdoms of the Spirit. Perhaps it arrives at its object, but only to fall asleep in the Infinite. Or, if it remains awake, it is in the highest experience of the Supreme into which the self-annulling Mind can enter, but not in the supreme of the Supreme, *parātpara*. The Mind can only be aware of the Self in a mentalised spiritual thinness, only of the mind-reflected Sachchidananda. The highest truth, the integral self-knowledge is not to be gained by this self-blinded leap into the Absolute but by a patient transit beyond the mind into the Truth-Consciousness where the Infinite can be known, felt, seen, experienced in all the fullness of its unending riches."[21]

* That which is supreme over Buddhi is He. (Ed.)

The Psychic Being and Transformation

In spiritual experience there exists one sole Being, one sole Existence which embraces all beings and existing things in the universe, and which in spiritual realisation is experienced as the One Self of all things and creatures. But in our ordinary experience we perceive the world as inhabitated by a plurality of beings and things existing outside what we felt to be our self. This is because our true self, described previously as the Purusha, who is one with the Self of all things and beings, has identified itself through ignorance with Prakriti, its outer instrumental nature made up of body, life and mind. This identification of Purusha with Prakriti has led to the formation in us of an ego — physical, vital and mental — which gives us the sense of a self that is separate from the rest of the universe. Thus it is the ego that gives rise to the distinction ingrained in our ordinary consciousness between what we feel to be our self and the rest of the universe which is perceived as the not-self. Also, it is the ego — physical, vital and mental — which, due to its complexity and heterogeneity, leads to the formation of multiple selves or personalities, causing division, conflict, disharmony and disorganisation in our outer being. Harmonisation and unification of the outer being can be brought about only by discovering our inmost being — Chaitya Purusha or the psychic being — and organising the outer being around the psychic as its centre and governing principle.

The aim of spiritual quest in the past has generally been to obtain liberation from the bondage to suffering caused by the illusory sense of a separate self, the ego, and thereby escape from the perpetual cycle of birth and death. According to Sri Aurobindo, the farther goal of spiritual evolution beyond liberation consists in the transformation of the instruments of the spirit — mind, life and body — so as to establish the kingdom of the spirit on earth. It is when the outer being is unified and governed by the psychic being that the transformation of mind, life and body becomes possible. As Sri Aurobindo states:

> "The psychic being... supports the mind, vital, body, grows by their experiences, carries the nature from life to life.... At first it is veiled by mind, vital and body, but as it grows, it becomes capable of coming forward and dominating the mind, life and body; in the ordinary man it depends on them for expression and is not able to take them up and freely use them. The life of the being is animal or human and not divine. When the psychic being can by sadhana become dominant and freely use its instruments, then the impulse towards the Divine becomes complete and the transformation of mind, vital and body, not merely their liberation, becomes possible."[22]

A.S. Dalal

REFERENCES

(All the following references pertain to Sri Aurobindo's works.)

1. *The Life Divine — Book Two Part Two*, Sri Aurobindo Birth Centenary Library (SABCL) (Pondicherry: Sri Aurobindo Ashram, 1970-73), Vol. 19, p. 897.

2. *Letters on Yoga — Part One* (SABCL, Vol. 22), p. 303.
3. *The Synthesis of Yoga — Parts One and Two* (SABCL, Vol. 20), pp. 68-69.
4. *Ibid.*, p. 68.
5. *Letters on Yoga — Parts Two and Three* (SABCL, Vol. 23), p. 1019-20.
6. *Letters on Yoga — Part One,* p. 251.
7. *Ibid.*, p. 320.
8. *Letters on Yoga — Part Four* (SABCL, Vol. 24), p. 1602.
9. *Letters on Yoga — Part One,* pp. 313-14.
10. *The Life Divine — Book One and Book Two Part One* (SABCL, Vol. 18), pp. 225-26.
11. *The Life Divine — Book Two Part Two*, pp. 733-34.
12. *The Life Divine — Book One and Book Two Part One,* p. 550.
13. *Letters on Yoga — Part One*, p. 360.
14. *The Future Poetry*, (SABCL, Vol. 9), p. 342.
15. *The Life Divine — Book Two Part Two*, p. 944.
16. *Ibid.*, pp. 946-47.
17. *Letters on Yoga — Part One*, p. 244.
18. *The Life Divine — Book One and Book Two Part One*, pp. 278-79.
19. *The Supramental Manifestation* (SABCL, Vol. 16), pp. 41-42.
20. *The Synthesis of Yoga — Parts One and Two*, p. 395.
21. *Ibid.*, p. 281.
22. *Letters on Yoga — Part One*, p. 283.

1

OUR MANIFOLD BEING

A psychical* self-knowledge tells us that there are in our being many formal, frontal, apparent or representative selves and only one that is entirely secret and real; to rest in the apparent and to mistake it for the real is the one general error, root of all others and cause of all our stumbling and suffering, to which man is exposed by the nature of his mentality.[1]

— SRI AUROBINDO

*

The ordinary human being is conscious only in his physical being, and only in relatively rare moments is he conscious of his mind, just a little more frequently of his vital, but all this is mixed up in his consciousness, so much so that he would be quite unable to say, "This movement comes from the mind, this from the vital, this from the physical." This already asks for a considerable development in order to be able to distinguish within oneself the source of the different movements one has. And it is so mixed that even when one tries, at the beginning it is very difficult to classify and separate one thing from another.

It is as when one works with colours, takes three or four or five different colours and puts them in the same water and beats them up together, it makes a grey, indistinct and in-

---

* "Psychical" here means "inner" or "deeper". – (Ed.)

comprehensible mixture, you see, and one can't say which is red, which blue, which green, which yellow; it is something dirty, lots of colours mixed. So first of all one must do this little work of separating the red, blue, yellow, green — putting them like this, each in its corner. It is not at all easy.

I have met people who used to think themselves extremely intelligent, by the way, who thought they knew a lot, and when I spoke to them about the different parts of the being they looked at me like this (*gesture*) and asked me, "But what are you speaking about?" They did not understand at all. I am speaking of people who have the reputation of being intelligent. They don't understand at all. For them it is just the consciousness; it is the consciousness — "It is my consciousness" and then there is the neighbour's consciousness; and again there are things which do not have any consciousness. And then I asked them whether animals had a consciousness; so they began to scratch their head and said, "Perhaps it is we who put our consciousness in the animal when we look at it," like that...[2]   — THE MOTHER

*

"It is part of the foundation of Yoga to become conscious
of the great complexity of our nature, see the different
forces that move it and get over it a control of directing
knowledge."   — Sri Aurobindo

Are these forces different for each person?

Yes. The composition is completely different, otherwise

everybody would be the same. There are not two beings with an identical combination; between the different parts of the being and the composition of these parts the proportion is different in each individual. There are people, primitive men, people like the yet undeveloped races or the degenerated ones whose combinations are fairly simple; they are still complicated, but comparatively simple. And there are people absolutely at the top of the human ladder, the élite of humanity; their combinations become so complicated that a very special discernment is needed to find the relations between all these things.

There are beings who carry in themselves thousands of different personalities, and then each one has its own rhythm and alternation, and there is a kind of combination; sometimes there are inner conflicts, and there is a play of activities which are rhythmic and with alternations of certain parts which come to the front and then go back and again come to the front. But when one takes all that, it makes such complicated combinations that some people truly find it difficult to understand what is going on in themselves; and yet these are the ones most capable of a complete, coordinated, conscious, organised action; but their organisation is infinitely more complicated than that of primitive or undeveloped men who have two or three impulses and four or five ideas, and who can arrange all this very easily in themselves and seem to be very co-ordinated and logical because there is not very much to organise. But there are people truly like a multitude, and so that gives them a plasticity, a fluidity of action and an extraordinary complexity of perception, and these people are capable of understanding a considerable number of things, as though they had at their disposal a veritable army which they move according to circumstance and need; and all this is inside them. So when these people, with the help of yoga, the discipline of yoga, succeed in centralising all these beings around the central light of the divine Presence, they become powerful entities, precisely because of their complexity. So long as this is not organised they often give the impression of an incoherence, they are almost incomprehensible, one can't manage to understand why they are like that, they are so complex. But when they have organised all these beings, that is, put each one in its place around the divine centre, then truly they are terrific, for they have the capacity of understanding almost everything and doing almost everything because of the multitude of entities they contain, of which they are constituted. And the nearer one is to the summit of the ladder, the more is it like that, and consequently the more difficult is it to organise one's being; because when you have about a dozen elements, you can quickly compass and organise them, but when you have thousands of them, it is difficult.[3] — THE MOTHER

*

Men do not know themselves and have not learned to distinguish the different parts of their being; for these are usually lumped together by them as mind, because it is through a mentalised perception and understanding that they know or feel them; therefore they do not understand their own states and actions, or, if at all, then only on the surface. It is part of the foundation of yoga to become conscious of the great complexity of our nature, see the different forces that move it and get over it a control of directing knowledge. We are composed of many parts each of which contributes something to the total movement of our consciousness, our thought, will, sensation, feeling, action, but we do not see the origination or the course of these impulses; we are aware only of their confused and pell-mell results on the surface upon which we can at best impose nothing better than a precarious shifting order.[4]   — SRI AUROBINDO

*

... man is not made up of one piece but of many pieces and each part of him has a personality of its own. That is a thing which people yet have not sufficiently realised — the psychologists have begun to glimpse it, but recognise only when there is a marked case of double or multiple personality. But all men are like that, in reality.[5] — SRI AUROBINDO

*

The ordinary mind knows itself only as an ego with all the movements of the nature in a jumble and, identifying itself with these movements, thinks "I am doing this, feeling that, thinking, in joy or in sorrow etc." The first beginning of real self-knowledge is when you feel yourself separate from the nature in you and its movements and then you see that there are many parts of your being, many personalities each acting on its own behalf and in its own way.[6]

— SRI AUROBINDO

*

... your being is full of innumerable tendencies at war with one another — almost different personalities, we may say. When one of them gives itself to the Divine, the others come up and refuse their allegiance. "We have not given ourselves," they cry, and start clamouring for their independence and expression. Then you bid them be quiet and show them the Truth. Patiently you have to go round your whole being, exploring each nook and corner, facing all those anarchic elements in you which are waiting for their psychological moment to come up. And it is only when you have made the entire round of your mental, vital and physical nature, persuaded everything to give itself to the Divine and thus achieved an absolute unified consecration that you put an end to your difficulties. Then indeed yours is a glorious walk towards transformation, for you no longer go from darkness to knowledge but from knowledge to knowledge, light to light, happiness to happiness....[7]   — THE MOTHER

*

An "entity" is a personality or an individuality. There are many such "personalities" in each one of us. If these personalities agree and are complementary with one another, they make up a human being, a rich and complex "person". But that is not what usually happens. These personalities do not agree with one another. For example, one of them might wish to make some progress, to become more and more perfect, to get a deeper knowledge of things, to realise more and more, to proceed towards the perfection of the being, while another one may simply want to have fun and enjoy itself as much as it can; one day it will do this, the next day something else, etc. If the personalities do not agree, this person's life will be incoherent, and that is not unusual: in fact, these cases are very common....

What happens then? Conflicts, friction, inner disorder created by these individualities which are unable to get on with one another. The strongest one gets the upper hand; it is not only dominant over the others but curbs them to stop them from rebelling. So, in the end, the unlucky ones, the repressed ones, go to sleep. They bide their time, and when that time comes, they suddenly jump up and turn everything upside down. If that happens very often, that person's life will be a very disorderly one. He will take up one thing today and go on with another tomorrow and so on.[8] — THE MOTHER

*

You say that it is necessary to establish "homogeneity in our being"?

Don't you know what a homogeneous thing is, made up of all similar parts? That means the whole being must be under the same influence, same consciousness, same tendency, same will. We are formed of all kinds of different pieces. They become active one after another. According to the part that is active, one is quite another person, becomes almost another personality. For instance, one had an aspiration at first, felt that everything existed only for the Divine, then something happens, somebody comes along, one has to do something, and everything disappears. One tries to recall

the experience, not even the memory of the experience remains. One is completely under another influence, one wonders how this could have happened. There are examples of
double, triple, quadruple personalities, altogether unconscious of themselves.... But it is not about this I am speaking; I am speaking about something which has happened to
all of you: you have had an experience, and for some time
you have felt, understood that this experience was the only
thing that was important, that had an absolute value — half
an hour later you try to recall it, it is like a smoke that van-
ishes. The experience has disappeared. And yet half an hour
ago it was there and so powerful.... It is because one is made
of all kinds of different things. The body is like a bag with
pebbles and pearls all mixed up, and it is only the bag which
keeps all that together. This is not a homogeneous, uniform
consciousness but a heterogeneous one.[9]   — THE MOTHER

*

The practice of Yoga brings us face to face with the extraordinary complexity of our own being, the stimulating but also
embarrassing multiplicity of our personality, the rich endless confusion of Nature. To the ordinary man who lives
upon his own waking surface, ignorant of the self's depths
and vastnesses behind the veil, his psychological existence
is fairly simple. A small but clamorous company of desires,
some imperative intellectual and aesthetic cravings, some
tastes, a few ruling or prominent ideas amid a great current
of unconnected or ill-connected and mostly trivial thoughts,
a number of more or less imperative vital needs, alternations of physical health and disease, a scattered and incon-

sequent succession of joys and griefs, frequent minor disturbances and vicissitudes and rarer strong searchings and
upheavals of mind or body, and through it all Nature, partly
with the aid of his thought and will, partly without or in
spite of it, arranging these things in some rough practical
fashion, some tolerable disorderly order, — this is the material of his existence. The average human being even now is
in his inward existence as crude and undeveloped as was the
bygone primitive man in his outward life. But as soon as we
go deep within ourselves, — and Yoga means a plunge into
all the multiple profundities of the soul, — we find ourselves
subjectively, as man in his growth has found himself objectively, surrounded by a whole complex world which we have
to know and to conquer.

The most disconcerting discovery is to find that every part
of us — intellect, will, sense-mind, nervous or desire self,
the heart, the body — has each, as it were, its own complex
individuality and natural formation independent of the rest;
it neither agrees with itself nor with the others nor with the
representative ego which is the shadow cast by some central
and centralising self on our superficial ignorance. We find
that we are composed not of one but many personalities and
each has its own demands and differing nature. Our being is
a roughly constituted chaos into which we have to introduce
the principle of a divine order.[10]   — SRI AUROBINDO

*

... why then are we not normally aware of so much that is
behind us and always pressing upon us? For the same reason that we are not aware of the inner life of our neighbour,

although it exists as much as our own and is constantly exercising an occult influence upon us, — for a great part of our thoughts and feelings come into us from outside, from our fellow-men, both from individuals and from the collective mind of humanity; and for the same reason that we are not aware of the greater part of our own being which is subconscient or subliminal to our waking mind and is always influencing and in an occult manner determining our surface existence. It is because we use, normally, only our corporeal senses and live almost wholly in the body and the physical vitality and the physical mind, and it is not directly through these that the life-world enters into relations with us. That is done through other sheaths of our being, — so they are termed in the Upanishads, — other bodies, as they are called in a later terminology, the mental sheath or subtle body in which our true mental being lives and the life sheath or vital body which is more closely connected with the physical or food-sheath and forms with it the gross body of our complex existence. These possess powers, senses, capacities which are always secretly acting in us, are connected with and impinge upon our physical organs and the plexuses of our physical life and mentality. By self-development we can become aware of them, possess our life in them, get through them into conscious relation with the life-world and other worlds and use them also for a more subtle experience and more intimate knowledge of the truths, facts and happenings of even the material world itself. We can by this self-development live more or less fully on planes of our existence other than the material which is now all in all to us.[11]   — SRI AUROBINDO

2

PLANES AND PARTS OF THE BEING

... first we must understand what we mean by planes of consciousness, planes of existence. We mean a general settled poise or world of relations between Purusha and Prakriti, between the Soul and Nature. For anything that we can call world is and can be nothing else than the working out of a general relation which an universal existence has created or established between itself, or let us say its eternal fact or potentiality and the powers of its becoming. That existence in its relations with and its experience of the becoming is what we call soul or Purusha, individual soul in the individual, universal soul in the cosmos; the principle and the powers of the becoming are what we call Nature or Prakriti.[12]
— SRI AUROBINDO

*

The universal Purusha dwells in all these planes in a certain simultaneity and builds upon each of these principles a world or series of worlds with its beings who live in the nature of that principle. Man, the microcosm, has all these planes in his own being, ranged from his subconscient to his superconscient existence. By a developing power of Yoga he can become aware of these concealed worlds hidden from his physical, materialised mind and senses which know only the material world, and then he becomes aware that his material existence is not a thing apart and self-existent, as the material universe in which he lives is also not a thing apart

and self-existent, but is in constant relation to the higher
planes and acted on by their powers and beings. He can open
up and increase the action of these higher planes in himself
and enjoy some sort of participation in the life of the other
worlds, — which, for the rest, are or can be his dwelling-
place, that is to say, the station of his awareness....[13]

SRI AUROBINDO

*

The physical is not the only world; there are others that we
become aware of through dream records, through the subtle
senses, through influences and contacts, through imagination, intuition and vision. There are worlds of a larger subtler life than ours, vital worlds; worlds in which Mind builds
its own forms and figures, mental worlds; psychic worlds
which are the soul's home; others above with which we have
little contact. In each of us there is a mental plane of consciousness, a psychic, a vital, a subtle physical as well as
the gross physical and material plane. The same planes are
repeated in the consciousness of general Nature. It is when
we enter or contact these other planes that we come into
connection with the worlds above the physical. In sleep we
leave the physical body, only a subconscient residue remaining, and enter all planes and all sorts of worlds. In each we
see scenes, meet beings, share in happenings, come across
formations, influences, suggestions which belong to these
planes. Even when we are awake, part of us moves in these
planes, but their activity goes on behind the veil; our waking minds are not aware of it.[14]   — SRI AUROBINDO

*

As we progress and awaken to the soul in us and things, we shall realise that there is a consciousness also in the plant, in the metal, in the atom, in electricity, in everything that belongs to physical nature; we shall find even that it is not really in all respects a lower or more limited mode than the mental, on the contrary it is in many "inanimate" forms more intense, rapid, poignant, though less evolved towards the surface. But this also, this consciousness of vital and physical Nature is, compared with Chit, a lower and therefore a limited form, mode and movement. These lower modes of consciousness are the conscious-stuff of inferior planes in one indivisible existence. In ourselves also there is in our subconscious being an action which is precisely that of the "inanimate" physical Nature whence has been constituted the basis of our physical being, another which is that of plant-life, and another which is that of the lower animal creation around us. All these are so much dominated and conditioned by the thinking and reasoning conscious-being in us that we have no real awareness of these lower planes; we are unable to perceive in their own terms what these parts of us are doing, and receive it very imperfectly in the terms and values of the thinking and reasoning mind. Still we know well enough that there is an animal in us as well as that which is characteristically human, — something which is a creature of conscious instinct and impulse, not reflective or rational, as well as that which turns back in thought and will on its experience, meets it from above with the light and force of a higher plane and to some degree controls, uses and modifies it. But the animal in man is only the head of our subhuman being; below it there is much that is also sub-animal and merely vital, much that acts by an instinct and impulse of which the constituting consciousness is withdrawn behind the surface. Below this sub-animal being, there is at a further depth the subvital. When we advance in that ultra-normal self-knowledge and experience which Yoga brings with it, we become aware that the body too has a consciousness of its own; it has habits, impulses, instincts, an inert yet effective will which differs from that of the rest of our being and can resist it and condition its effectiveness. Much of the struggle in our being is due to this composite existence and the interaction of these varied and heterogeneous planes on each other. For man here is the result of an evolution and contains in himself the whole of that evolution up from the merely physical and subvital conscious being to the mental creature which at the top he is.

But this evolution is really a manifestation and just as we have in us these subnormal selves and subhuman planes, so are there in us above our mental being supernormal and superhuman planes.[15]   — SRI AUROBINDO

The Physical

Each plane of our being — mental, vital, physical — has its own consciousness, separate though interconnected and interacting; but to our outer mind and sense, in our waking experience, they are all confused together....

There is the universal physical consciousness of Nature and there is our own which is a part of it, moved by it, and used by the central being for the support of its expression in the physical world and for a direct dealing with all these external objects and movements and forces. This physical consciousness-plane receives from the other planes their powers and influences and makes formations of them in its own province. Therefore we have a physical mind as well as a vital mind and the mind proper; we have a vital-physical part in us — the nervous being — as well as the vital proper; and both are largely conditioned by the gross material bodily part which is almost entirely subconscient to our experience.[16]

SRI AUROBINDO

*

Everything has a physical part — even the mind has a physical part; there is a mental physical, a mind of the body and the material. So the emotional being has a physical part. It has no location separate from the rest of the emotional. One can only distinguish that when the consciousness becomes sufficiently subtle to do so.[17]   — SRI AUROBINDO

*

By the gross physical is meant the earthly and bodily physical — as experienced by the outward sense-mind and senses. But that is not the whole of Matter. There is a subtle physical also with a subtler consciousness in it which can, for instance, go to a distance from the body and yet feel and be aware of things in a not merely mental or vital way.[18]

SRI AUROBINDO

*

The physical nerves are part of the material body but they are extended into the subtle body and there is a connection between the two.[19]   — SRI AUROBINDO

*

The vital physical, on the other hand, is the vehicle of the nervous responses of our physical nature; it is the field and instrument of the smaller sensations, desires, reactions of all kinds to the impacts of the outer physical and gross material life. This vital physical part (supported by the lowest part of the vital proper) is therefore the agent of most of the lesser movements of our external life; its habitual reactions and obstinate pettinesses are the chief stumbling-block in the way of transformation of the outer consciousness by the yoga. It is also largely responsible for most of the suffering and disease of mind or body to which the physical being is subject in Nature.[20]   — SRI AUROBINDO

*

The vital body surrounds the physical body with a kind of envelope which has almost the same density as the vibrations of heat observable when the day is very hot. And it is this which is the intermediary between the subtle body and the most material vital body. It is this which protects the body from all contagion, fatigue, exhaustion and even from accidents. Therefore if this envelope is wholly intact, it protects you from everything, but a little too strong an emotion, a little fatigue, some dissatisfaction or any shock whatsoever is sufficient to scratch it as it were and the slightest scratch allows any kind of intrusion. Medical science also now recognises that if you are in perfect vital equilibrium, you do not catch illness or in any case you have a kind of immunity from contagion. If you have this equilibrium, this inner harmony which keeps the envelope intact, it protects you from everything. There are people who lead quite an ordinary life, who know how to sleep as one should, eat as one should, and their nervous envelope is so intact that they pass through all dangers as though unconcerned. It is a capacity one can cultivate in oneself. If one becomes aware of the weak spot in one's envelope, a few minutes' concentration, a call to the force, an inner peace is sufficient for it to be all right, get cured, and for the untoward thing to vanish.[21]

THE MOTHER

*

All illnesses pass through the nervous or vital-physical sheath of the subtle consciousness and subtle body before they enter the physical. If one is conscious of the subtle body or with the subtle consciousness, one can stop an illness on its way and prevent it from entering the physical body. But it may have come without one's noticing, or when one is asleep or through the subconscient, or in a sudden rush when one is off one's guard; then there is nothing to do but to fight it out from a hold already gained on the body.[22]

SRI AUROBINDO

*

That is how illnesses try to come from one person to another — they attack, by a suggestion like this or otherwise, the nervous being and try to come in. Even if the illness is not contagious, this often happens, but it comes more easily in contagious illnesses. The suggestion or touch has to be thrown off at once.

There is a sort of protection round the body which we call the nervous envelope — if this remains strong and refuses entrance to the illness force, then one can remain well even in the midst of plague or other epidemics — if the envelope is pierced or weak, then the illness can come in.[23]

SRI AUROBINDO

*

They [the subtle forces of illness] first weaken or break through the nervous envelope, the aura. If that is strong and whole, a thousand million germs will not be able to do anything to you. The envelope pierced, they attack the subconscient mind in the body, sometimes also the vital mind or mind proper — prepare the illness by fear or thought of illness. The doctors themselves say that in influenza or cholera in the Far East 90 p.c. get ill through fear. Nothing to take away the resistance like fear.[24]

SRI AUROBINDO

*

What are the causes of accidents? Are they due to a disequilibrium?

If one answers deeply... Outwardly there are many causes, but there is a deeper cause which is always there. I said the other day that if the nervous envelope is intact, accidents can be avoided, and even if there is an accident it won't have any consequences. As soon as there is a scratch or a defect in the nervous envelope of the being and according to the nature of this scratch, if one may say so, its place, its character, there will be an accident which will correspond to the diminution of resistance in the envelope. I believe almost everybody is psychologically aware of one thing: that accidents occur when one has a sort of uncomfortable feeling, when one is not fully conscious and self-possessed, when one feels uneasy. In any case, generally, people have a feeling that they are not fully themselves, not fully aware of what they are doing. If one were fully conscious, the consciousness wide awake, accidents would not occur; one would make just the right gesture, the necessary movement to avoid the accident. Hence, in an almost absolute way, it is a flagging of consciousness. Or quite possibly it may be that the consciousness is fixed in a higher domain; for example, not to speak of spiritual things, a man who is busy solving a mental problem and is very concentrated upon his mental problem, becomes inattentive to physical things, and if he happens to be in a street or in a crowd, his attention fixed upon his problem, he will not make the movement necessary to avoid the accident, and the accident will occur. It is the same for sports, for games; you can observe this easily, there is always a flagging of the consciousness when accidents occur, or a lack of attention, a little absent-mindedness; suddenly one thinks of something else, the attention is drawn elsewhere — one is not fully conscious of what one is doing and the accident happens.

As I was telling you at the beginning, if for some reason or other — for example, lack of sleep, lack of rest or an absorbing preoccupation or all sorts of things which tire you, that is to say, when you are not above them — if the vital envelope is a little damaged, it does not function perfectly and any current of force whatever which passes through is enough to produce an accident. In the final analysis, the accident comes always from that, it is what one may call inattentiveness or a slackening of consciousness. There are days when one feels quite... not exactly uneasy, but as though one were trying to catch something which escapes, one can't hold together, one is as though half-diluted; these are the days of accidents. You must be attentive. Naturally, this is not to tell you to shut yourself up in your room and not to stir out when you feel like that! This is not what I mean. Rather I mean that you must watch all the more attentively, be all the more on your guard, not allow, precisely, this inattentiveness, this slackening of consciousness to come in.[25]   — THE MOTHER

*

The body... has its own consciousness and acts from it, even without any mental will of our own or even against that will, and our surface mind knows very little about this body-consciousness, feels it only in an imperfect way, sees only its results and has the greatest difficulty in finding out their causes. It is part of the yoga to become aware of this separate consciousness of the body, to see and feel its movements and the forces that act upon it from inside or outside and to learn how to control and direct it even in its most hidden and (to us) subconscient processes. But the body-consciousness itself is only part of the individualised physical consciousness in us which we gather and build out of the secretly conscious forces of universal physical Nature.[26]

SRI AUROBINDO

*

... the body obeys the mind automatically in those things in which it is formed or trained to obey it, but the relation of the body to the mind is not in all things that of an automatic perfect instrument. The body also has a consciousness of its own and, though it is a submental instrument or servant consciousness, it can disobey or fail to obey as well. In many things, in matters of health and illness for instance, in all automatic functionings, the body acts on its own and is not a servant of the mind. If it is fatigued, it can offer a passive resistance to the mind's will. It can cloud the mind with tamas, inertia, dullness, fumes of the subconscient so that the mind cannot act. The arm lifts, no doubt, when it gets the suggestion, but at first the legs do not obey when they are asked to walk; they have to learn how to leave the crawling attitude and movement and take up the erect and ambulatory habit. When you first ask the hand to draw a straight line or to play music, it can't do it and won't do it. It has to be schooled, trained, taught, and afterwards it does automatically what is required of it. All this proves that there is a body-consciousness which can do things at the mind's order, but has to be awakened, trained, made a good and conscious instrument. It can even be so trained that a mental will or suggestion can cure the illness of the body.[27]

SRI AUROBINDO

*

There is a consciousness in the cells: it is what we call the "body consciousness" and it is wholly bound up with the body. This consciousness has much difficulty in changing, because it is under the influence of the collective suggestion which is absolutely opposed to the transformation. So one has to struggle with this collective suggestion, not only with the collective suggestion of the present, but with the collective suggestion which belongs to the earth-consciousness as a whole, the terrestrial human consciousness which goes back to the earliest formation of man. That has to be overcome before the cells can be spontaneously aware of the Truth, of the Eternity of matter.

Of course, until now, those who have achieved this conscious transformation, who are aware of the eternal and infinite life within themselves, in the depths of their being, must, in order to preserve this consciousness, constantly refer back to their inner experience, return to their inner contemplation, live in a sort of more or less constant meditation. And when they come out of meditation, their outer nature is pretty much what it was before, and their way of thinking and reacting is not very different — unless they give up action altogether. But in that case the inner realisation, this transformation of the consciousness, is helpful only for the person who has achieved it, but it doesn't change the condition of matter or earthly life in the least.

For this transformation to succeed, all human beings —
even all living beings as well as their material environment
— must be transformed. Otherwise things will remain as they
are: an individual experience cannot change terrestrial life.
This is the essential difference between the old idea of transformation — that is, the becoming conscious with the psychic being and the inner life — and transformation as we
conceive it and speak of it. Not only an individual or a group
of individuals or even all individuals, but life, the overall
consciousness of this more or less developed material life,
have to be transformed. Without such a transformation we
shall have the same misery, the same calamities and the same
atrocities in the world. A few individuals will escape from it
by their psychic development, but the general mass will remain in the same state of misery.[28]   — THE MOTHER

*

... in the body, for instance, when there is something like an
attack, an accident, an illness trying to come in — something — an attack on the body, a body that is left to its natural spontaneity has an urge, an aspiration, a spontaneous will
to call for help. But as soon as the affair goes to the head, it
takes the form of things to which one is accustomed: everything is spoilt. But if the body is seen in itself, just as it is,
there is something which suddenly wakes up and calls for
help, and with such a faith, such an intensity, just as the tiny
little baby calls its mamma, you know — or whoever is
there, it says nothing if it cannot speak. But the body left to
itself without this kind of constant action of the mind upon

it... well, it has this: as soon as there is some disturbance, immediately it has an aspiration, a call, an effort to seek help, and this is very powerful. If nothing intervenes, it is very powerful. It is as though the cells themselves sprang up in an aspiration, a call.

In the body there are invaluable and unknown treasures. In all its cells, there is an intensity of life, of aspiration, of the will to progress which one does not usually even realise. The body-consciousness would have to be completely warped by the action of the mind and vital for it not to have an immediate will to reestablish the equilibrium. When this will is not there, it means that the entire body-consciousness has been spoilt by the intervention of the mind and vital. In people who cherish their malady more or less subconsciously with a sort of morbidity under the pretext that it makes them interesting, it is not their body at all — poor body! — it is something they have imposed upon it with a mental or vital perversion. The body, if left to itself, is remarkable, for, not only does it aspire for equilibrium and well-being but it is capable of restoring the balance. If one leaves one's body alone without intervening with all those thoughts, all the vital reactions, all the depressions, and also all the so-called knowledge and mental constructions and fears — if one leaves the body to itself, spontaneously it will do what is necessary to set itself right again.

The body in its natural state likes equilibrium, likes harmony; it is the other parts of the being which spoil everything.[29]   — THE MOTHER

*

How should we come out of the physical consciousness which keeps us preoccupied all the time and exclusively with physical circumstances?

There is a considerable number of ways.

There are intellectual ways, ways which may be called sentimental, artistic ways and spiritual ways. And generally, it is preferable for each one to take the way that is easiest for him, for if one wants to begin straight away with the most difficult, one comes to nothing at all. And here we always come back to the same thing, to what Sri Aurobindo describes in *The Synthesis of Yoga*: it is the way of knowledge or the way of devotion or the way of works. But the way of works is precisely the one which keeps you in physical life and makes you find your liberation in it; and perhaps this is the most effective way of all but also the most difficult.

For most aspirants the way of meditation, concentration, withdrawal from physical life, rejection of physical activities is certainly easier than the way of action. But they leave the physical consciousness just as it is, without ever changing it, and unless one becomes like a sadhu or an ascetic who leaves behind all active life and remains in constant concentration or meditation, one achieves nothing at all. That is to say, an entire part of the being is never transformed. And for them the solution is not at all to transform it, it is simply to reject it, to get out of their body as quickly as possible. That is how yoga was conceived of formerly, for, obviously, it is much easier. But this is not what we want.

What we want is the transformation of the physical consciousness, not its rejection.

And so, in this case, what Sri Aurobindo has recommended as the most direct and most total way is surrender to the Divine — a surrender made more and more integral, progressively, comprising the physical consciousness and physical activities. And if one succeeds in this, then the physical, instead of being an obstacle, becomes a help.[30]

THE MOTHER

The Vital

Vital... is a thing of desires, impulses, force-pushes, emotions, sensations, seekings after life-fulfilment, possession and enjoyment; these are its functions and its nature; — it is that part of us which seeks after life and its movements for their own sake and it does not want to leave hold of them if they bring it suffering as well as or more than pleasure; it is even capable of luxuriating in tears and suffering as part of the drama of life. What then is there in common between the thinking intelligence and the vital and why should the latter obey the mind and not follow its own nature? The disobedience is perfectly normal instead of being, as Augustine suggests, unintelligible. Of course, man can establish a mental control over his vital and in so far as he does it he is a man, — because the thinking mind is a nobler and more enlightened entity and consciousness than the vital and ought, therefore, to rule and, if the mental will is strong, can rule. But this rule is precarious, incomplete and held only by much self-discipline. For if the mind is more enlightened, the vital is nearer to earth, more intense, vehement, more directly able to touch the body. There is too a vital mind which lives by imagination, thoughts of desire, will to act and enjoy from its own impulse and this is able to seize on the reason itself and make it its auxiliary and its justifying counsel and supplier of pleas and excuses. There is also the sheer force of Desire in man which is the vital's principal support and strong enough to sweep off the reason, as the Gita says, "like a boat on stormy waters".[31]

SRI AUROBINDO

*

"All or most of the works of life are at present or seem to be actuated or vitiated by the soul of desire; even those that are ethical or religious, even those that wear the guise of altruism, philanthropy, self-sacrifice, self-denial, are shot through and through with the threads of its making. This soul of desire is a separative soul of ego and all its instincts are for a separative self-affirmation; it pushes always, openly or under more or less shining masks, for its own growth, for possession, for enjoyment, for conquest and empire."   — Sri Aurobindo, *The Synthesis of Yoga*

Sweet Mother, what is the "soul of desire"?

It is what makes you live, act, move.

Soul, the word for soul in French, "*âme*" comes from a word which means "to animate". It is what gives life to the body. If you didn't have it you would be inert matter, something like stones or plants, not altogether inert, but vegetative.

Some people say that without desires, that is, without this soul of desire, there would never have been any progress.... In ordinary life it is something very useful but when one decides to do yoga, to find the Divine, it becomes a little cumbersome.[32]   — THE MOTHER

*

... the vital soul is what animates the body, the life which animates the body. You see, in ordinary language it is said, "You die when your soul leaves your body" or "Your soul leaves your body when you die", in one way or the other; but it is not the soul, it is not only this soul — what we call soul, I mean the psychic being — it is the vital being. When the vital being leaves the body for whatever reason, the body dies or death cuts off the vital being from the body.... So it is in the sense of animating, that is, giving life.

Is this the "vital desire-soul", Sweet Mother?

Yes, the vital soul is full of desires. The vital being is full of desires. It is built of desires.[33]   — THE MOTHER

*

One must refuse pleasure if one wants to open to the delight of existence, in a total beauty and harmony.

This brings us quite naturally to vital austerity, the austerity of the sensations, the tapasya of power. For the vital being is the seat of power, of effective enthusiasm. It is in the vital that thought is transformed into will and becomes a dynamism for action. It is also true that the vital is the seat of desires and passions, of violent impulses and equally violent reactions, of revolt and depression. The normal remedy is to strangle and starve the vital by depriving it of all sensation; sensations are indeed its main sustenance and without them it falls asleep, grows sluggish and starves to death.

In fact, the vital has three sources of subsistence. The one most easily accessible to it comes from below, from the physical energies through the sensations.

The second is on its own plane, when it is sufficiently vast and receptive, by contact with the universal vital forces.

The third, to which it usually opens only in a great aspiration for progress, comes to it from above by the infusion and absorption of spiritual forces and inspiration.

To these sources men always strive more or less to add another, which is for them at the same time the source of most of their torments and misfortunes. It is the interchange of vital forces with their fellows, usually in groups of two, which they most often mistake for love, but which is only the attraction between two forces that take pleasure in mutual interchange.

Thus, if we do not wish to starve our vital, sensations must not be rejected or diminished in number and intensity. Neither should we avoid them; rather we must make use of them with wisdom and discernment. Sensations are an excellent instrument of knowledge and education, but to make them serve these ends, they must not be used egoistically for the sake of enjoyment, in a blind and ignorant search for pleasure and self-satisfaction.

The senses should be capable of enduring everything without disgust or displeasure, but at the same time they must acquire and develop more and more the power of discerning the quality, origin and effect of the various vital vibrations in order to know whether they are favourable to harmony, beauty and good health or whether they are harmful to the balance and progress of the physical being and the vital. Moreover, the senses should be used as instruments to approach and study the physical and vital worlds in all their complexity; in this way they will take their true place in the great endeavour towards transformation.

It is by enlightening, strengthening and purifying the vital, and not by weakening it, that one can contribute to the true progress of the being. To deprive oneself of sensations is therefore as harmful as depriving oneself of food. But just as the choice of food must be made wisely and solely for the growth and proper functioning of the body, so too the choice of sensations and their control should be made with a very scientific austerity and solely for the growth and perfection of the vital, of this highly dynamic instrument, which is as essential for progress as all the other parts of the being.

It is by educating the vital, by making it more refined, more sensitive, more subtle and, one should almost say, more elegant, in the best sense of the word, that one can overcome its violence and brutality, which are in fact a form of crudity and ignorance, of lack of taste.

In truth, a cultivated and illumined vital can be as noble and heroic and disinterested as it is now spontaneously vulgar, egoistic and perverted when it is left to itself without education. It is enough for each one to know how to transform in himself the search for pleasure into an aspiration for the supramental plenitude. If the education of the vital is carried far enough, with perseverance and sincerity, there comes a time when, convinced of the greatness and beauty of the goal, the vital gives up petty and illusory sensorial satisfactions in order to win the divine delight.[34]

THE MOTHER

*

Most people live in the vital. That means that they live in their desires, sensations, emotional feelings, vital imaginations and see and experience and judge everything from that point of view. It is the vital that moves them, the mind being at its service, not its master. In yoga also many people do sadhana from that plane and their experience is full of vital visions, formations, experiences of all kinds, but there is no mental clarity or order, neither do they rise above the mind. It is only the minority of men who live in the mind or in the psychic or try to live in the spiritual plane.[35]

SRI AUROBINDO

*

In the ordinary life people accept the vital movements, anger, desire, greed, sex, etc. as natural, allowable and legitimate things, part of the human nature. Only so far as society discourages them or insists to keep them within fixed limits or subject to a decent restraint or measure, people try to control them so as to conform to the social standard of morality or rule of conduct. Here, on the contrary, as in all spiritual life, the conquest and complete mastery of these things is demanded.[36]   — SRI AUROBINDO

*

Does depression come from the vital?

Oh, yes. All your troubles, depression, discouragement, disgust, fury, all, all come from the vital. It is that which turns love into hate, it is that which induces the spirit of vengeance, rancour, bad will, the urge to destroy and to harm. It is that which discourages you when things are difficult and not to its liking. And it has an extraordinary capacity for going on strike! When it is not satisfied, it hides in a corner and does not budge. And then you have no more energy, no more strength, you have no courage left. Your will is like... like a withering plant. All resentment, disgust, fury, all despair, grief, anger — all that comes from this gentleman. For it is energy in action.

Therefore, it depends on which side it turns. And I tell you, it has a very strong habit of going on strike. That is its most powerful weapon: "Ah! you are not doing what I want, well, I am not going to move, I shall sham dead." And it does that for the least reason. It has a very bad character; it is very touchy and it is very spiteful — yes, it is very ill-natured. For I believe it is very conscious of its power and it feels clearly that if it gives itself wholly, there is nothing that will resist the momentum of its force. And like all people who have a weight in the balance, the vital also bargains: "I shall give you my energy, but you must do what I want. If you do not give me what I ask for, well, I withdraw my energy." And you will be flat as a pancake. And it is true, it happens like that.

It is difficult to regulate it. Yet naturally, when you have succeeded in taming it, you have something powerful in hand for realisation. It is that which can carry by storm the biggest obstacles. It is that which is capable of turning an idiot into an intelligent person — it alone can do so; for if one yearns passionately for progress, if the vital takes it into its head that one must progress, even the greatest idiot can become intelligent! I have seen this, I am not speaking from hearsay; I have seen it, I have seen people who were dull, stupid, incapable of understanding, who understood nothing — you could go on explaining something to them for months, it would not enter, as though one were speaking to a block of wood — and then all of a sudden their vital was caught in a passion; they wanted simply to please someone or get something, and for that one had to understand, one had to know, it was necessary. Well, they set everything moving, they shook up the sleeping mind, they poured energy into all the corners where there was none; and they understood, they became intelligent. I knew someone who knew nothing practically, understood nothing, and who, when the mind started moving and the passion for progress took possession of him, began to write wonderful things. I have them with me. And when the movement withdrew, when the vital went on strike (for sometimes it went on strike, and withdrew), the person became once again absolutely dull.

Naturally it is very difficult to establish a constant contact between the most external physical consciousness and the psychic consciousness, and oh! the physical consciousness has plenty of goodwill; it is very regular, it tries a great deal, but it is slow and heavy, it takes long, it is difficult to move it. It does not get tired, but it makes no effort; it goes its way, quietly. It can take centuries to put the external consciousness in contact with the psychic. But for some reason or other the vital takes a hand in it. A passion seizes it. It wants this contact (for some reason or other, which is not always a spiritual reason), but it wants this contact. It wants it with all its energy, all its strength, all its passion, all its fervour: in three months the thing is done.

So then, take great care of it. Treat it with great consideration but never submit to it. For it will drag you into all kinds of troublesome and untoward experiments; and if you succeed in convincing it in some way or other, then you will advance with giant strides on the path.[37]   — THE MOTHER

*

Sweet Mother, is desire contagious?

Ah, yes, very contagious, my child. It is even much more contagious than illness. If someone next to you has a desire, immediately it enters you; and in fact it is mainly in this way that it is caught. It passes from one to another... Terribly contagious, in such a powerful way that one is not even aware that it is a contagion. Suddenly one feels something springing up in oneself; someone has gently put it inside. Of course, one could say, "Why aren't people with desires

quarantined?" Then we should have to quarantine everybody. (*Mother laughs*)[38] — THE MOTHER

*

"Will, Power, Force are the native substance of the Life-
Energy, and herein lies the justification for the refusal of
Life to acknowledge the supremacy of Knowledge and
Love alone, — for its push towards the satisfaction of something far more unreflecting, headstrong and dangerous that
can yet venture too in its own bold and ardent way towards the Divine and Absolute. Love and Wisdom are not
the only aspects of the Divine, there is also its aspect of
Power." — Sri Aurobindo, *The Synthesis of Yoga*

... Sri Aurobindo says that the vital part, the vital being is
the greatest obstacle because it is unregenerate, and that
there would be a possibility of transforming it if it surrendered entirely to Love and Knowledge; but as its predominant quality is force, energy, power, it does not like to submit
to other parts of the being, and this justifies its refusal to
submit itself, for those virtues in their essence are as high as
the others. That is why it has neither the same power nor the
same capacities, for it is not developed, it has not surrendered, and this is what causes the dilemma: it does not submit because it has this power, and this power cannot be
utilised because it is not surrendered. So, how to get out of
that? The vital, if it were surrendered, would be a very powerful help, extremely useful, it would make the whole process go much more rapidly. But because it feels its own

power, it refuses to submit to the others; and because it does not submit, its power cannot be utilised. So, what is to be done? Sri Aurobindo states the problem — he is going to solve it afterwards; if we continue reading, after a while he will tell us how to solve this problem — but he states it first so that we may fully understand the situation.

If the vital were a mediocre being without definite qualities, there would be no difficulty in its surrendering, but it would be altogether useless. But, on the contrary, the vital is a sort of stronghold of energy and power — of all powers. Yet generally this power is diverted; it is no longer at the service of the Divine, it is at the service of the vital itself for its own satisfaction. So, as long as it is like that, it cannot be used.

It should come to understand that this energy and power which it feels within itself cannot become useful unless it enters into perfect harmony with the divine plan of realisation on earth. If it understands that, it becomes quiet and allows itself to be enlisted, so to say, in the totality of the being, and then it takes on its full strength and full importance. But otherwise, it cannot be used. And usually, all its activities are activities which always complicate things and take away their simplicity, their purity, often their beauty, and their effectiveness, for its action is blind, ignorant and very egoistic.[39]   — THE MOTHER

*

As there is a physical mind, so there is a physical vital — a vital turned entirely upon physical things, full of desires and greeds and seekings for pleasure on the physical plane.

The physical-vital is the being of small desires and greeds, etc. — the vital-physical is the nervous being; they are closely connected together.

The vital-physical governs all the small daily reactions to outward things — reactions of the nerves and the body consciousness and the reflex emotions and sensations; it motives much of the ordinary actions of man and joins with the lower parts of the vital proper in producing lust, jealousy, anger, violence etc. In its lowest parts (vital-material) it is the agent of pain, physical illness etc.

Yes — they [the lower vital, the physical vital and the most material vital] become very clear to the increasing consciousness. And the distinctions are necessary — otherwise one may influence or control the lower vital or a part of the physical vital and then be astonished to find that something intangible but apparently invincible still resists — it is the material vital with so much of the rest as it can influence by its resistance.

The nervous part of the being is a portion of the vital — it is the vital-physical, the life-force closely enmeshed in the reactions, desires, needs, sensations of the body.[40]

SRI AUROBINDO

The Mental

The "Mind" in the ordinary use of the word covers indiscriminately the whole consciousness, for man is a mental being and mentalises everything; but in the language of this yoga the words "mind" and "mental" are used to connote specially the part of the nature which has to do with cognition and intelligence, with ideas, with mental or thought perceptions, the reactions of thought to things, with the truly mental movements and formations, mental vision and will, etc., that are part of his intelligence. The vital has to be carefully distinguished from mind, even though it has a mind element transfused into it; the vital is the Life-nature made up of desires, sensations, feelings, passions, energies of action, will of desire, reactions of the desire-soul in man and of all that play of possessive and other related instincts, anger, fear, greed, lust, etc., that belong to this field of the nature. Mind and vital are mixed up on the surface of the consciousness, but they are quite separate forces in themselves and as soon as one gets behind the ordinary surface consciousness one sees them as separate, discovers their distinction and can with the aid of this knowledge analyse their surface mixtures. It is quite possible and even usual during a time shorter or longer, sometimes very long, for the mind to accept the Divine or the yogic ideal while the vital is unconvinced and unsurrendered and goes obstinately on its way of desire, passion and attraction to the ordinary life. Their division or their conflict is the cause of most of the more acute difficulties of the sadhana.[41] — SRI AUROBINDO

*

... people usually think that mind is just a mode of activity, whereas there is a mental substance as there is a vital substance and physical substance. And as there is a substance, there is a corresponding world with an autonomous existence, that is to say, there can be a mind without any physical support. The physical body may disappear and the mind can continue to exist. It is here that it is important to understand that there is a mental substance which, obviously, is much more... (*silence*) how to put it?... immaterial than physical matter.

Some people use a rather unclassical word, "rarefied", but I don't think it has exactly this sense. Well, you see, we say that substance has different densities, and the more material it becomes, the denser it is, the farther it moves away from matter, the less dense it is. But it is a substance all the same. There is even an etheric substance. I don't say that this conforms with scientific theories; I don't guarantee that I am not talking scientific heresies! But this is a cosmic fact. (*Mother laughs.*) It is exactly — I think I said this when I spoke about occultism — I said the first thing one must know before being able to practise occultism is that the different states of being have a different density, and they have an individual independent existence of their own, that they are existing realities, that they are truly real substances, that it is not just a way of being. There can be a mental being and mental activity and, for instance, a thought that is completely independent of the brain, whereas the materialistic theories say that it is the brain which creates mental activity. But this is not correct. The brain is the material transcription of the mental activity, and mental activity has its own domain; the mental domain has its reality, its own substance. One can think outside one's brain, think, act, make formations outside one's brain. One can even live, move, go from one place to another, have a direct knowledge of mental things in the mental world, in a word, absolutely independent of a body which, indeed, can be in a state of complete inertia, not only asleep but also in a cataleptic state. And moreover, it is quite certain that so long as one has not understood that one is made up of different states of being which have their own independent life, one can't have a complete control over one's being. There will always be something that escapes you.[42]

THE MOTHER

*

... the true role of the mind is the formation and organisation of action. The mind has a formative and organising power, and it is that which puts the different elements of inspiration in order, for action, for organising action. And if it would only confine itself to that role, receiving inspirations — whether from above or from the mystic centre of the soul — and simply formulating the plan of action — in broad outline or in minute detail, for the smallest things of life or the great terrestrial organisations — it would amply fulfil its function.

It is not an instrument of knowledge.

But it can use knowledge for action, to organise action. It is an instrument of organisation and formation, very powerful and very capable when it is well developed.

One can feel this very clearly when one wants to organise one's life, for instance — to put the different elements in their place in one's existence. There is a certain intellectual faculty which immediately puts each thing in its place and makes a plan and organises. And it is not a knowledge that comes from the mind, it is a knowledge which comes, as I said, from the mystic depths of the soul or from a higher consciousness; and the mind concentrates it in the physical world and organises it to give a basis of action to the higher consciousness.

One has this experience very clearly when one wants to organise one's life.

Then, there is another use. When one is in contact with one's reason, with the rational centre of the intellect, the pure reason, it is a powerful control over all vital impulses. All that comes from the vital world can be very firmly controlled by it and used in a disciplined and organised action. But it must be at the service of something else — not work for its own satisfaction.

These are the two uses of the mind: it is a controlling force, an instrument of control, and it is a power of organisation. That is its true place.[43]   — THE MOTHER

*

Is reason the highest function of the mind?

Of the mind properly speaking, of the human mind, yes, certainly. That is, with the reason one doesn't risk making mistakes, as long as one remains in the purely human and purely mental domain.

How can reason become an obstacle to the spiritual life?

Because it understands nothing about it. Spiritual life goes beyond it, it is not its domain, and it doesn't understand anything there. It is a very good instrument for all ethics, morality, self-control, but spiritual life goes beyond these things and reason understands nothing of it.

> *But if one truly has reason, then reason has to admit*
> *that the spiritual life is higher!*

Yes.

> *Then why does it become an obstacle?*

On condition that it keeps quiet, does not intervene any more... if it tries to intervene it is an obstacle, if it withdraws in an orderly way and remains quiet, then it is very good.

It is an obstacle if you want to use it as judge and master. But it is not an obstacle if you use it as an instrument, like all the other parts of the being. It is an excellent instrument on condition that it remains an instrument and doesn't want to become the master who decides and judges. It is a power of judgment which, in its field, is absolutely right. But as soon as it goes beyond its domain, it cannot understand, it has no discernment any longer.

So if the reason understands this and keeps quiet, with the attitude of an instrument and not of master and judge, it is perfect. But for this the growing consciousness must already be developed enough in a suprarational domain to be able to act on the reason from above and make it understand the thing, because that domain is not a part of reason. So naturally it denies it unless there is a part of the consciousness which is sufficiently developed to be able to put something upon it that will make it understand. All depends on the degree of development of the individual's consciousness.[44]

THE MOTHER

*

"Late, I learned that when reason died then Wisdom was born; before that liberation, I had only knowledge."

Sri Aurobindo, *Thoughts and Aphorisms*

Once again I must repeat that the form of these aphorisms is purposely paradoxical in order to give the mind a little shock and awaken it enough for it to make an effort to understand. One must not take this aphorism literally. Some people seem worried by the idea that reason must disappear for one to become wise. It is not that, it is not that at all.

Reason must no longer be the summit and the master.

For a very long time in life, until one possesses anything resembling Knowledge, it is indispensable that reason be the master, otherwise one is the plaything of one's impulses, one's fancies, one's more or less disordered emotional imaginings, and one is in danger of being very far removed not merely from wisdom but even from the knowledge needed for conducting oneself acceptably. But when one has managed to control all the lower parts of the being with the help of reason, which is the apex of ordinary human intelligence, then if one wants to go beyond this point, if one wants to liberate oneself from ordinary life, from ordinary thought, from the ordinary vision of things, one must, if I may say so, stand upon the head of reason, not trampling it down disdainfully,

but using it as a stepping stone to something higher, something beyond it, to attain to something which concerns itself
very little with the decrees of reason; something which can
allow itself to be irrational because it is a higher irrationality,
with a higher light; something which is beyond ordinary
knowledge and which receives its inspirations from above,
from high above, from the divine Wisdom.

That is what this means.

As for the knowledge of which Sri Aurobindo speaks here,
it is ordinary knowledge, it is not Knowledge by identity; it
is knowledge that can be acquired by the intellect through
thought, through ordinary means.

But once again — and in any case we shall have occasion
to return to this when we study the next aphorism — do not
be in a hurry to abandon reason in the conviction that you
will immediately attain to Wisdom, because you must be
ready for Wisdom; otherwise, by abandoning reason, you run
a great risk of falling into unreason, which is rather dangerous.

Many times in his writings, particularly in *The Synthesis
of Yoga*, Sri Aurobindo warns us against the imaginings of
those who believe they can do sadhana without rigorous self-
control and who heed all sorts of inspirations, which lead
them to a dangerous imbalance where all their repressed, hidden, secret desires come out into the open under the pre-
tence of liberation from ordinary conventions and ordinary
reason.

One can be free only by soaring to the heights, high above
human passions. Only when one has achieved a higher, self-

less freedom and done away with all desires and impulses does one have the right to be free.

But neither should people who are very reasonable, very moral according to ordinary social laws, think themselves wise, for their wisdom is an illusion and holds no profound truth.

One who would break the law must be above the law. One who would ignore conventions must be above conventions. One who would despise all rules must be above all rules. And the motive of this liberation should never be a personal, egoistic one: the desire to satisfy an ambition, aggrandise one's personality, through a feeling of superiority, out of contempt for others, to set oneself above the herd and regard it with condescension. Be on your guard when you feel yourself superior and look down on others ironically, as if to say, "I'm no longer made of such stuff." That's when you go off the track and are in danger of falling into an abyss.

When one truly attains wisdom, the true wisdom, the wisdom Sri Aurobindo is speaking of here, there is no longer higher and lower; there is only a play of forces in which each thing has its place and its importance. And if there is a hierarchy it is a hierarchy of surrender to the Supreme. It is not a hierarchy of superiority with regard to what is below.

And with human understanding, human reason, human knowledge, one is unable to discern this hierarchy. Only the awakened soul can recognise another awakened soul, and then the sense of superiority disappears completely.

True wisdom comes only when the ego disappears, and the ego disappears only when you are ready to abandon your-

self completely to the supreme Lord without any personal
motive and without any expectation of profit — when you
do it because you cannot do otherwise.[45]   — THE MOTHER

*

There is a part of the nature which I have called the vital
mind; the function of this mind is not to think and reason, to
perceive, consider and find out or value things, for that is
the function of the thinking mind proper, *buddhi*, — but to
plan or dream or imagine what can be done. It makes formations for the future which the will can try to carry out if
opportunity and circumstances become favourable or even
it can work to make them favourable. In men of action this
faculty is prominent and a leader of their nature; great men
of action always have it in a very high measure. But even if
one is not a man of action or practical realisation or if circumstances are not favourable or one can do only small and
ordinary things, this vital mind is there. It acts in them on a
small scale, or if it needs some sense of largeness, what it
does very often is to plan in the void, knowing that it cannot
realise its plans or else to imagine big things, stories, adven-
tures, great doings in which oneself is the hero or the crea-
tor. What you describe as happening in you is the rush of
this vital mind or imagination making its formations; its
action is not peculiar to you but works pretty much in the
same way in most people — but in each according to his
turn of fancy, interest, favourite ideas or desires. You have
to become master of its action and not to allow it to seize
your mind and carry it away when and where it wants. In

sadhana when the experiences begin to come, it is exceedingly important not to allow this power to do what it likes with you; for it then creates false experiences according to its nature and persuades the sadhak that these experiences are true or it builds unreal formations and persuades him that this is what he has to do. Some have been taken away by this misleading force used by powers of Falsehood who persuaded them through it that they had a great spiritual, political or social work to do in the world and led them away to disappointment and failure.[46]   — SRI AUROBINDO

*

The vital mind is that part of the vital being which builds, plans, imagines, arranges things and thoughts according to the life-pushes, desires, will to power or possession, will to action, emotions, vital ego reactions of the nature. It must be distinguished from the reasoning will which plans and arranges things according to the dictates of the thinking mind proper, the discriminating reason or according to the mental intuition or a direct insight and judgment. The vital mind uses thought for the service not of reason but of life-push and life-power and when it calls in reasoning it uses that for justifying the dictates of these powers, imposes their dictates on the reason instead of governing by a discriminating will the action of the life-forces.[47]

SRI AUROBINDO

*

The true thinking mind does not belong to the physical, it is a separate power. The physical mind is that part of the mind which is concerned with the physical things only — it depends on the sense-mind, sees only objects, external actions, draws its ideas from the data given by external things, infers from them only and knows no other Truth until it is enlightened from above.[48]   — SRI AUROBINDO

*

The physical mind is that which is fixed on physical objects and happenings, sees and understands these only, and deals with them according to their own nature, but can with difficulty respond to the higher forces. Left to itself, it is sceptical of the existence of supraphysical things, of which it has no direct experience and to which it can find no clue; even when it has spiritual experiences, it forgets them easily, loses the impression and result and finds it difficult to believe. To enlighten the physical mind by the consciousness of the higher spiritual and supramental planes is one object of this yoga, just as to enlighten it by the power of the higher vital and higher mental elements of the being is the greatest part of human self-development, civilisation and culture.[49]

SRI AUROBINDO

*

One of the chief functions of the physical mind is to doubt. If you listen to it, it will always find a thousand reasons for doubting. But you must know that the physical mind is working in ignorance and full of falsehoods.[50]

THE MOTHER

*

Sweet Mother, is the physical mind the same as the mechanical mind?

Almost. You see, there is just a little difference, but not much. The mechanical mind is still more stupid than the physical mind. The physical mind is what we spoke about one day, that which is never sure of anything.

I told you the story of the closed door, you remember. Well, that is the nature of the physical mind. The mechanical mind is at a lower level still, because it doesn't even listen to the possibility of a convincing reason, and this happens to everyone. Usually we don't let it function, but it comes along repeating the same things, absolutely mechanically, without rhyme or reason, just like that. When some craze or other takes hold of it, it goes... For example, you see, if it fancies counting: "One, two, three, four", then it will go on: "One, two, three, four; one, two, three, four." And you may think of all kinds of things, but it goes on: "One, two, three, four", like that... (*Mother laughs.*) Or it catches hold of three words, four words and repeats them and goes on repeating them; and unless one turns away with a certain violence and punches it soundly, telling it, "Keep quiet!", it continues in this way, indefinitely.[51]   — THE MOTHER

*

The mechanical mind is a sort of engine — whatever comes to it it puts into the machine and goes on turning it round and round no matter what it is.

That is the nature of the mental physical to go on repeating without use the movement that has happened. It is what we call the mechanical mind — it is strong in childhood because the thinking mind is not developed and has besides a narrow range of interests. Afterwards it becomes an under-current in the mental activities.[52]   — SRI AUROBINDO

The Subconscient

What does "subconscient" mean, exactly?

Subconscient? It is what is half conscious, you see. And we say "sub", because that means "below" the consciousness. It is something more obscure than the consciousness, but which, at the same time, is like a lower substratum supporting the consciousness. It is like those stores from which one would draw out something quite unformed, a formless substance which could be translated into forms or translated into actions or translated into impulses or even into feelings. But it is like those stores containing a considerable number of fairly mixed things, not very distinct, but which would be very rich in possibilities; only they would have to be drawn out into the light and organised, classified, put into shape so as to give them a value.

So long as they are there, it is a mass, a mixture, certainly subconscient, that is to say, half-conscious, semi-conscious, in which everything is muddled up. It lacks organisation and classification. It is the characteristic of consciousness to organise and classify... classification, putting into order, arranging logically... there are varieties of logic, but still, some logic, a beginning of logic. There are higher and higher kinds of logic, more and more superior. But even preliminary logic is the first work of the consciousness.

But consciousness is plunged — plunged as though by its roots — into this domain, and draws up as it would draw up sap; it constantly pumps this subconscient which it has to transform into something organised. That is why we spend our time re-doing the same work. If we had a small limited amount of consciousness which was our own, as some people imagine it, like a small bag full of consciousness, you know, which is one's own consciousness, well, when you have put it in good order and organised it well, your work will be done, and you can be quiet. But it is not at all like that, it is not at all like that.

Even as there are elements of consciousness which escape and evaporate, which spread out, there is this constant rising, as from a deep ground, of something that asks to be made conscious. And your work has to be perpetually re-done. But one can — if one is careful and attentive — instead of re-doing exactly the same thing each time, one can re-do it with a little progress. Then the movement is not rectilinear, but a movement which goes like this... you see (*gesture of spiral movement*). One seems at times to be going back, but that's in order to go farther and farther forward.[53]

THE MOTHER

*

Sweet Mother, is the subconscient stronger than the mind, vital and physical?

... It has a greater power. Well, just because it is subconscient it is everywhere, everything seems steeped in the subconscient. And so, "subconscient" means half conscious: not conscious and not unconscious. It is just between the two; it is like that, half-way; so things slide down into it, one doesn't know that they are there, and from there they act; and it is because one doesn't know that they are there that they can remain there. There are many things which one doesn't wish to keep and drives out from the active consciousness, but they go down there, hide there, and because it is subconscious one doesn't notice them; but they haven't gone out completely, and when they have a chance to come up again, they come up. For example, there are bad habits of the body, in the sense that the body is in the habit of upsetting its balance — we call that falling ill, you know; but still, the functioning becomes defective through a bad habit. You manage by concentrating the Force and applying it on this defect, to make it disappear but it doesn't disappear completely, it enters the subconscient. And then, when you are off your guard, when you stop paying attention properly and preventing it from showing itself, it rises up and comes out. You thought for months perhaps or even for years, you thought you were completely rid of a certain kind of illness which you suffered from, and you no longer paid any attention, and suddenly one day it returns as though it had never gone; it springs up again from the subconscient and unless one enters into this subconscient and changes things there, that is, unless one changes the subconscient into the conscient, it always happens like this. And the method is to change the subconscient into the conscient — if each thing that rises to the surface becomes conscious, at that moment it must be changed. There is a more direct method still: it is to enter the subconscient in one's full consciousness and work there, but this is difficult. Yet so long as this is not done, all the progress one has made — I mean physically, in one's body — can always be undone.[54]   — THE MOTHER

*

... we mean by the subconscient that quite submerged part of our being in which there is no wakingly conscious and coherent thought, will or feeling or organized reaction, but which yet receives obscurely the impressions of all things and stores them up in itself and from it too all sorts of stimuli, of persistent habitual movements, crudely repeated or disguised in strange forms can surge up into dream or into the waking nature. For if these impressions rise up most in dream in an incoherent and disorganized manner, they can also and do rise up into our waking consciousness as a mechanical repetition of old thoughts, old mental, vital and physical habits or an obscure stimulus to sensations, actions, emotions which do not originate in or from our conscious thought or will and are even often opposed to its perceptions, choice or dictates. In the subconscient there is an obscure mind full of obstinate Sanskaras, impressions, associations, fixed notions, habitual reactions formed by our past, an obscure vital full of the seeds of habitual desires, sensations and nervous reactions, a most obscure material which governs much that has to do with the condition of the body. It is largely responsible for our illnesses; chronic or repeated illnesses are indeed mainly due to the subconscient and its obstinate memory and habit of repetition of whatever has impressed itself upon the body-consciousness. But this subconscient must be clearly distinguished from the subliminal parts of our being such as the inner or subtle physical consciousness, the inner vital or inner mental; for these are not at all obscure or incoherent or ill-organized, but only veiled from our surface consciousness. Our surface constantly receives something, inner touches, communications or influences, from these sources but does not know for the most part whence they come.[55]   — SRI AUROBINDO

*

The subconscient is universal as well as individual like all the other main parts of the Nature. But there are different parts or planes of the subconscient. All upon earth is based on the Inconscient as it is called, though it is not really inconscient at all, but rather a complete "sub"-conscience, a suppressed or involved consciousness, in which there is everything but nothing is formulated or expressed. The subconscient lies between this Inconscient and the conscious mind, life and body. It contains the potentiality of all the primitive reactions to life which struggle out to the surface from the dull and inert strands of Matter and form by a constant development a slowly evolving and self-formulating consciousness; it contains them not as ideas, perceptions or conscious reactions but as the fluid substance of these things. But also all that is consciously experienced sinks down into the subconscient, not as precise though submerged memories but as obscure yet obstinate impressions of experience, and these can come up at any time as dreams, as mechanical repetitions of past thought, feelings, action, etc., as "complexes" exploding into action and event, etc., etc. The subconscient is the main cause why all things repeat themselves and nothing ever gets changed except in appearance. It is the cause why people say character cannot be changed, the cause also of the constant return of things one hoped to have got rid of for ever. All seeds are there and all Sanskaras of the mind, vital and body, — it is the main support of death and disease and the last fortress (seemingly impregnable) of the Ignorance. All too that is suppressed without being wholly got rid of sinks down there and remains as seed ready to surge up or sprout up at any moment.[56]   — SRI AUROBINDO

*

About the subconscient — it is the sub-mental base of the being and is made up of impressions, instincts, habitual movements that are stored there. Whatever movement is impressed in it, it keeps. If one impresses the right movement in it, it will keep and send up that. That is why it has to be cleared of old movements before there can be a permanent and total change in the nature. When the higher consciousness is once established in the waking parts, it goes down into the subconscient and changes that also, makes a bedrock of itself there also. Then no further trouble from the subconscient will be possible. But even before that one can minimise the trouble by putting the right will and the right habit of reaction in the subconscient parts.[57]

SRI AUROBINDO

*

As there is a superconscient (something above our present consciousness) above the head from which the higher consciousness comes down into the body, so there is also a subconscient (something below our consciousness) below the feet. Matter is under the control of this power, because it is that out of which it has been created — that is why matter seems to us to be quite unconscious. The material body is very much under the influence of this power for the same reason; it is why we are not conscious of what is going on in the body, for the most part. The outer consciousness goes down into this subconscient when we are asleep, and so it becomes unaware of what is going on in us when we are asleep except for a few dreams. Many of these dreams rise up from the subconscient and are made up of old memories, impressions etc. put together in an incoherent way. For the subconscient receives impressions of all we do or experience in our lives and keeps these impressions in it, sending up often fragments of them in sleep. It is a very important part of the being, but we can do nothing much with it by the conscious will. It is the higher Force working in us that in its natural course will open the subconscient to itself and bring down into it its control and light.[58]

SRI AUROBINDO

*

Can one learn to control one's subconscient as one controls one's conscious thought?

It is especially during the body's sleep that one is in contact with the subconscient. In becoming conscious of one's nights, control of the subconscient becomes much easier.

The control can become total when the cells become conscious of the Divine in them and when they open themselves voluntarily to His influence.[59]   — THE MOTHER

*

It is quite normal for difficulties to come back... and it is not a proof that no progress has been made. The recurrence (after one has thought one has conquered) is not unaccountable. I have explained in my writings what happens. When a habitual movement long embedded in the nature is cast out, it takes refuge in some less enlightened part of the nature, and when cast out of the rest of the nature, it takes refuge in the subconscient and from there surges up when you least expect it or comes up in dreams or sudden inconscient movements or it goes out and remains in wait in the environmental being through which the universal Nature works and attacks from there as a force from outside trying to recover its kingdom by a suggestion or repetition of old movements. One has to stand fast till the power of return fades away. These returns or attacks must be regarded not as parts of oneself, but as invasions — and rejected without allowing any depression or discouragement. If the mind does not sanction them, if the vital refuses to welcome them, if the physical remains steady and refuses to obey the physical urge, then the recurrence of the thought, the vital impulse, the physical feeling will begin to lose its last holds and finally they will be too feeble to cause any trouble.[60]

SRI AUROBINDO

The Inconscient

... in its actual cosmic manifestation the Supreme, being the
Infinite and not bound by any limitation, can manifest in
Itself, in its consciousness of innumerable possibilities,
something that seems to be the opposite of itself, something
in which there can be Darkness, Inconscience, Inertia, In-
sensibility, Disharmony and Disintegration. It is this that we
see at the basis of the material world and speak of nowadays
as the Inconscient — the Inconscient Ocean of the Rigveda
in which the One was hidden and arose in the form of this
universe — or, as it is sometimes called, the non-being, Asat.
The Ignorance which is the characteristic of our mind and
life is the result of this origin in the Inconscience. Moreover, in the evolution out of inconscient existence there rise
up naturally powers and beings which are interested in the
maintenance of all negations of the Divine, error and unconsciousness, pain, suffering, obscurity, death, weakness,
illness, disharmony, evil. Hence the perversion of the manifestation here, its inability to reveal the true essence of the
Divine. Yet in this very base of this evolution all that is divine is there involved and pressing to evolve, Light, Consciousness, Power, Perfection, Beauty, Love. For in the
Inconscient itself and behind the perversions of the Ignorance the Divine Consciousness lies concealed and works
and must more and more appear, throwing off in the end its
disguises. That is why it is said that the world is called to
express the Divine.[61]   — SRI AUROBINDO

*

If one of you (I have my doubts, but still) went down into the Inconscient, what is called the pure Inconscient, you would realise what it is. A stone will seem to you a marvellously conscious object in comparison. You speak disdainfully of a stone because you have just a wee bit more consciousness than it has, but the difference between the consciousness of the stone and the total Inconscient is perhaps greater than that between the stone and you.[62]

THE MOTHER

*

We know by experience that if we go down into the subconscient, lower than the physical consciousness, into the subconscient and even lower still into the inconscient, we can find in ourselves the origin of atavism, of what comes from our early education and the environment in which we lived. And this gives a kind of special characteristic to the individual, to his outer nature, and it is generally believed that we are born like that and we will stay like that. But by going down into the subconscient, into the inconscient, one can trace the origin of this formation and undo what has been done, change the movements and reactions of the ordinary nature by a conscious and deliberate action and thus really transform one's character. This is not a common achievement, but it has been done. So one may assert not only that it can be done, but that it has been done. It is the first step towards the integral transformation....[63]

THE MOTHER

*

*Does the inconscient in oneself belong to the individual
being or to the earth?*

The inconscient is not individualised and when you go down
into the inconscient in yourself, it is the inconscient of
matter. One can't say that each individual has his own inconscient, for that would already be a beginning of individualisation, and when you go down into the inconscient,
it is perhaps not the universal but at least the terrestrial
inconscient.

The light, the consciousness that comes down into this
inconscient in order to transform it must necessarily be a
consciousness that is close enough to be able to touch it. It is
not possible to conceive of a light — the supramental light,
for example — that would have the power to individualise
the inconscient. But, through a conscious, individualised
being, this light can be brought down into the inconscient
and gradually make it conscious.

First of all, it is the subconscient that has to become conscious, and indeed the main difficulty of the integral transformation is that things are constantly rising up from the
subconscient. You think you have got a certain movement
under control — anger, for example. You try very hard to
control your anger and succeed to some extent, then suddenly it rises up again for some reason unknown to you, as if
you hadn't done anything at all, and you have to start all over
again. If it were the transformed part of the being going back
to its old ways, it would be most depressing, but it is not like
that. It is the material part, the material life which is sustained, supported, so to say, by a subconscient life. And this

subconscient is beginning to get individualised around some people; it has certain affinities with a kind of subconscient somewhat like our own, and that is where the things you have repressed or thrown out of your nature go to — and one fine day they rise up again. But if you are able to bring the light into the subconscient and make it conscious, this will no longer happen.[64]   — THE MOTHER

The Subliminal — The Inner Being

There is an inner as well as an outer consciousness all through our being, upon all its levels. The ordinary man is aware only of his surface self and quite unaware of all that is concealed by the surface. And yet what is on the surface, what we know or think we know of ourselves and even believe that that is all we are, is only a small part of our being and by far the larger part of us is below the surface. Or, more accurately, it is behind the frontal consciousness, behind the veil, occult and known only by an occult knowledge. Modern psychology and psychic science have begun to perceive this truth just a little. Materialistic psychology calls this hidden part the Inconscient, although practically admitting that it is far greater, more powerful and profound than the surface conscious self, — very much as the Upanishads called the superconscient in us the Sleep-self, although this Sleep-self is said to be an infinitely greater Intelligence, omniscient, omnipotent, Prajna, the Ishwara. Psychic science calls this hidden consciousness the subliminal self, and here too it is seen that this subliminal self has more powers, more knowledge, a freer field of movement than the smaller self that is on the surface. But the truth is that all this that is behind, this sea of which our waking consciousness is only a wave or series of waves, cannot be described by any one term, for it is very complex. Part of it is subconscient, lower than our waking consciousness, part of it is on a level with it but behind and much larger than it; part is above and superconscient to us. What we call our mind is only an outer mind, a surface mental action, instrumental for the partial expression of a larger mind behind of which we are not ordinarily aware and can only know by going inside ourselves. So too what we know of the vital in us is only the outer vital, a surface activity partially expressing a larger secret vital which we can only know by going within. Equally, what we call our physical being is only a visible projection of a greater and subtler invisible physical consciousness which is much more complex, much more aware, much wider in its receptiveness, much more open and plastic and free.

If you understand and experience this truth, then only you will be able to realise what is meant by the inner mental, the inner vital, the inner physical consciousness. But it must be noted that this term "inner" is used in two different senses. Sometimes it denotes the consciousness behind the veil of the outer being, the mental or vital or physical within, which is in direct touch with the universal mind, the universal life-forces, the universal physical forces. Sometimes, on the other hand, we mean an inmost mental, vital, physical, more specifically called the true mind, the true vital, the true physical consciousness which is nearer to the soul and can most easily and directly respond to the Divine Light and Power. There is no real yoga possible, still less any integral yoga, if we do not go back from the outer self and become aware of all this inner being and inner nature. For then alone can we break the limitations of the ignorant external self which receives consciously only the outer touches and knows things indirectly through the outer mind and senses, and become directly aware of the universal consciousness and the universal forces that play through us and around us. And then only too can we hope to be directly aware of the Divine in us and directly in touch with the Divine Light and the Divine Force. Otherwise we can feel the Divine only through external signs and external results and that is a difficult and uncertain way and very occasional and inconstant, and it leads only to belief and not to knowledge, not to the direct consciousness and awareness of the constant presence.[65]   — SRI AUROBINDO

*

There are, we might say, two beings in us, one on the surface, our ordinary exterior mind, life, body consciousness, another behind the veil, an inner mind, an inner life, an inner physical consciousness constituting another or inner self. This inner self once awake opens in its turn to our true real eternal self. It opens inwardly to the soul, called in the language of this yoga the psychic being which supports our successive births and at each birth assumes a new mind, life and body. It opens above to the Self or Spirit which is unborn and by conscious recovery of it we transcend the changing personality and achieve freedom and full mastery over our nature.[66]   — SRI AUROBINDO

*

... the subliminal in man is the largest part of his nature and has in it the secret of the unseen dynamisms which explain his surface activities. But the lower vital subconscious which is all that this psycho-analysis of Freud seems to know, — and even of that it knows only a few ill-lit corners, — is no more than a restricted and very inferior portion of the subliminal whole. The subliminal self stands behind and supports the whole superficial man; it has in it a larger and more efficient mind behind the surface mind, a larger and more powerful vital behind the surface vital, a subtler and freer physical consciousness behind the surface bodily existence. And above them it opens to higher superconscient as well as below them to lower subconscient ranges.[67]

SRI AUROBINDO

*

Sweet Mother, what does "the subliminal being" mean, exactly?

Well, it is what he [Sri Aurobindo] says, you know. It's what is behind. I think it is what could be called the subtle physical, the subtle vital, the subtle mind. It is something that's behind what is manifested. One can imagine that what is manifested is like a layer or like a crust or a bark; it is that which we see and with which we are in touch. And it clothes something, it clothes or expresses something which is more subtle and serves as its support.

When one dreams, one goes very often into his subliminal being, and there things are almost the same and yet not absolutely the same; there is a great resemblance and yet there is a difference; and usually this is greater. One has the impression of entering into something that's vaster; and, for example, one feels that one can do more, that one knows more, one has a power and clear-sightedness which one doesn't have in the ordinary consciousness; one has the impression while dreaming that one knows many more things than when one is awake.... when one dreams and knows a lot, for example, about the secret causes of things, about what a movement expresses... all that, one feels that one knows it. For instance, when one dreams of someone, one knows better what he thinks, what he wants, all these things, better than when one is in waking contact with him. This happens when one has entered the subliminal. Very often one dreams in the subliminal.[68]

THE MOTHER

*

It [the subliminal] is not necessarily more enlightened, more balanced — no. It is more subtle, it is less dull than our outer consciousness. Our external consciousness is so dull, it has no depth; as our outer understanding has no depth, our sensations have no depth; all this is something as though flat. So here it is fuller, but not necessarily more true.

Then why is it the most important?

Because it is internal. This is what supports the outer. The outer is only an appearance of this. As I said, in a dream when one goes there, one knows things which one doesn't know, one can do things, one is in touch with things which one doesn't know in the waking consciousness, because it is too superficial.

It is like the inside of something. The outside is the expression of that, but an altogether surface expression. So naturally it looks the same; in any case more than a resemblance, it has an identity with what we see of it from outside. We see the form, don't we, the expression; well, this expression has necessarily an analogy — more than an analogy — an identity with what is inside....

It is perhaps — perhaps — something like this, like the taste of a fruit. You know, you see a fruit, it has an appearance, it has a certain colour, it seems to you of a certain kind, but you cannot very well know what it tastes like until you taste it, that is, until you have entered inside it. It is something like this, something analogous to this.

Or maybe as in a watch — note that it is just to try to make myself understood, it is not really like that, it is only to try to make myself understood — when you see a watch, you see a dial and the hands moving, but if you want to know the watch you must open it and see the working inside.

It is something like that — you see only the effect, here; there is a cause behind. It is somewhat like that.

The world as we see it and our outer consciousness are the result of something which is behind, which Sri Aurobindo calls the subliminal. And this itself, as he says, is set in motion by impulses which come from the subconscient below and the superconscient above, and so it is as though it were assembled there, and once it is organised there it is expressed in the outer consciousness, the ordinary consciousness.

The best way is to go there; once you go there you understand what it is. And it is not difficult; one goes there constantly in dreams, very easily, without any effort.

How can we understand that we have gone there?

If you remember, you understand. If one remembers the kind of difference of impression one had: one has a certain impression, and when one returns one feels something like a disconnection, the impression is different, even the point of view one had about things is different. Well, if one remembers this, one understands. If one is in the habit, one can even while speaking or doing something, perceive very well — above all when speaking or thinking or reflecting on something — a second layer which is behind, much vaster, in which things are organised much more synthetically (not positively understandable) than in the outer consciousness. If one reflects just a little and looks at oneself thinking, one can see this at the back very well, one can see the two things moving together like this (*gesture*)... like the formulated thought and the source of the thought which is behind. And then when one thinks, you see, one has a feeling of being like this, enclosed in something; whereas, there, immediately one feels that one is in contact with many other things; and it is much greater.[69]   — THE MOTHER

*

... from there [subliminal forces] come all the greater aspirations, ideals, strivings towards a better self and better humanity without which man would be only a thinking animal — as also most of the art, poetry, philosophy, thirst for knowledge which relieve, if they do not yet dispel, the ignorance.[70]   — SRI AUROBINDO

*

Environmental Consciousness

The individual is not limited to the physical body — it is only the external consciousness which feels like that. As soon as one gets over this feeling of limitation, one can feel first the inner consciousness which is connected with the body, but does not belong to it, afterwards the planes of consciousness above the body, also a consciousness surrounding the body, but part of oneself, part of the individual being, through which one is in contact with the cosmic forces and with other beings. The last is what I have called the environmental consciousness.[71]   — SRI AUROBINDO

*

Each man has his own personal consciousness entrenched in his body and gets into touch with his surroundings only through his body and senses and the mind using the senses.

Yet all the time the universal forces are pouring into him without his knowing it. He is aware only of thoughts, feelings, etc., that rise to the surface and these he takes for his own. Really they come from outside in mind waves, vital waves, waves of feeling and sensation, etc., which take particular form in him and rise to the surface after they have got inside.

But they do not get into his body at once. He carries about with him an environmental consciousness (called by the Theosophists the Aura) into which they first enter. If you can become conscious of this environmental self of yours, then you can catch the thought, passion, suggestion or force of illness and prevent it from entering into you. If things in you are thrown out, they often do not go altogether but take refuge in this environmental atmosphere and from there they try to get in again. Or they go to a distance outside but linger on the outskirts or even perhaps far off, waiting till they get an opportunity to attempt entrance.[72]   — SRI AUROBINDO

*

When these things are rejected by the waking consciousness they try to take refuge in the subconscient or else in what may be called the environmental consciousness and from there they press upon the consciousness trying to recover their hold or simply to recur for a time. If they are in the subconscient they come up most usually in dreams, but they may also surge up into the waking consciousness. If they come from the environment they take the form of thought-suggestions or impulses or a vague restless or disturbing pressure.... When the body is full of the new consciousness, Peace and Power at the same time, then this outward pressure is felt but can no longer disturb and finally it recedes to a distance (no longer pressing immediately on the physical mind or body) and either gradually or rapidly disappears.

By environmental consciousness I mean something that each man carries around him, outside his body, even when he is not aware of it, — by which he is in touch with others and with the universal forces. It is through this that the thoughts, feelings etc. of others pass to enter into one — it is through this also that waves of the universal force — desire, sex, etc. come in and take possession of the mind, vital or body.[73]

SRI AUROBINDO

*

It is quite normal for difficulties to come back... and it is not a proof that no progress has been made. The recurrence (after one has thought one has conquered) is not unaccountable. I have explained in my writings what happens. When a habitual movement long embedded in the nature is cast out, it takes refuge in some less enlightened part of the nature, and when cast out of the rest of the nature, it takes refuge in the subconscient and from there surges up when you least expect it or comes up in dreams or sudden inconscient movements or it goes out and remains in wait in the environmental being through which the universal Nature works and attacks from there as a force from outside trying to recover its kingdom by a suggestion or repetition of old movements. One has to stand fast till the power of return fades away. These returns or attacks must be regarded not as parts of oneself, but as invasions — and rejected without allowing any depression or discouragement. If the mind does not sanction them, if the vital refuses to welcome them, if the physical remains steady and refuses to obey the physical urge, then the recurrence of the thought, the vital impulse, the physical feeling will begin to lose its last holds and finally they will be too feeble to cause any trouble.[74]

SRI AUROBINDO

The Superconscient

... there is a superconscient (something above our present consciousness) above the head from which the higher consciousness comes down into the body....[75]

SRI AUROBINDO

*

The higher consciousness is that above the ordinary mind and different from it in its workings; it ranges from higher mind through illumined mind, intuition and overmind up to the border line of the supramental.[76]   — SRI AUROBINDO

*

In this higher consciousness there are many degrees, of which the supramental is the summit or the source.[77]

SRI AUROBINDO

*

There are above us... successive states, levels or graded powers of being overtopping our normal mind, hidden in our own superconscient parts, higher ranges of Mind, degrees of spiritual consciousness and experience; without them there would be no links, no helpful intervening spaces to make the immense ascension possible. It is indeed from these higher sources that the secret spiritual Power acts upon the being and by its pressure brings about the psychic transformation or the spiritual change; but in the early stages of our growth this action is not apparent, it remains occult and unseizable.[78]

SRI AUROBINDO

*

... from the point of view of the ascent of consciousness from our mind upwards through a rising series of dynamic powers by which it can sublimate itself, the gradation can be resolved into a stairway of four main ascents, each with its high level of fulfilment. These gradations may be summarily described as a series of sublimations of the consciousness through Higher Mind, Illumined Mind and Intuition into Overmind and beyond it; there is a succession of self-transmutations at the summit of which lies the Supermind or Divine Gnosis.[79]

SRI AUROBINDO

*

Higher Mind

I mean by the Higher Mind a first plane of spiritual consciousness where one becomes constantly and closely aware of the Self, the One everywhere and knows and sees things habitually with that awareness; but it is still very much on the mind level although highly spiritual in its essential substance; and its instrumentation is through an elevated thought-power and comprehensive mental sight — not illumined by any of the intenser upper lights but as if in a large strong and clear daylight. It acts as an intermediate state between the Truth-Light above and the human mind; communicating the higher knowledge in a form that the Mind intensified, broadened, made spiritually supple, can receive without being blinded or dazzled by a Truth beyond it.[80] — SRI AUROBINDO

*

Illumined Mind

... greater Force [than that of the Higher Mind] is that of the Illumined Mind, a Mind no longer of higher Thought, but of spiritual light. Here the clarity of the spiritual intelligence, its tranquil daylight, gives place or subordinates itself to an intense lustre, a splendour and illumination of the Spirit: a play of lightnings of spiritual truth and power breaks from above into the consciousness and adds to the calm and wide enlightenment and the vast descent of peace which characterise or accompany the action of the larger conceptual-spiritual principle, a fiery ardour of realisation and a rapturous ecstasy of knowledge. A downpour of inwardly visible Light very usually envelops this action; for it must be noted that, contrary to our ordinary conceptions, light is not primarily a material creation and the sense or vision of light accompanying the inner illumination is not merely a subjective visual

image or a symbolic phenomenon: light is primarily a spiritual manifestation of the Divine Reality illuminative and creative; material light is a subsequent representation or conver-
sion of it into Matter for the purposes of the material Energy.
There is also in this descent the arrival of a greater dynamic,
a golden drive, a luminous "enthousiasmos" of inner force
and power which replaces the comparatively slow and deliberate process of the Higher Mind by a swift, sometimes a
vehement, almost a violent impetus of rapid transformation.[81]

SRI AUROBINDO

*

Intuition

The thought of the intuitive mind proceeds wholly by four
powers that shape the form of the truth, an intuition that suggests its idea, an intuition that discriminates, an inspiration
that brings in its word and something of its greater substance
and a revelation that shapes to the sight its very face and
body of reality. These things are not the same as certain movements of the ordinary mental intelligence that look analogous and are easily mistaken for the true intuition in our first
inexperience. The suggestive intuition is not the same thing
as the intellectual insight of a quick intelligence or the intuitive discrimination as the rapid judgment of the reasoning
intellect; the intuitive inspiration is not the same as the in-
spired action of the imaginative intelligence, nor the intuitive revelation as the strong light of a purely mental close
seizing and experience.

It would perhaps be accurate to say that these latter activities are mental representations of the higher movements, attempts of the ordinary mind to do the same things or the best possible imitations the intellect can offer of the functionings of the higher nature. The true intuitions differ from these effective but insufficient counterfeits in their substance of light, their operation, their method of knowledge. The intellectual rapidities are dependent on awakenings of the basic mental ignorance to mental figures and representations of truth that may be quite valid in their own field and for their own purpose but are not necessarily and by their very nature reliable. They are dependent for their emergence on the suggestions given by mental and sense data or on the accumulation of past mental knowledge. They search for the truth as a thing outside, an object to be found and looked at and stored as an acquisition and, when found, scrutinise its surfaces, suggestions or aspects. This scrutiny can never give a quite complete and adequate truth idea. However positive they may seem at the time, they may at any moment have to be passed over, rejected and found inconsistent with fresh knowledge.

The intuitive knowledge on the contrary, however limited it may be in its field or application, is within that scope sure with an immediate, a durable and especially a self-existent certitude.[82] — SRI AUROBINDO

*

To have the true intuition one must get rid of the mind's self-will, and the vital's also, their preferences, fancies, fantasies, strong insistences and eliminate the mental and vital ego's pressure which sets the consciousness to work in the service of its own claims and desires. Otherwise these things will come in with force and claim to be intuitions, inspirations and the rest of it. Or if any intuitions come, they can be twisted and spoiled by the mixture of these forces of the Ignorance.[83]   — SRI AUROBINDO

*

Overmind

Above the mind there are several levels of conscious being, among which the really divine world is what Sri Aurobindo has called the Supermind, the world of the Truth. But in between is what he has distinguished as the Overmind, the world of the cosmic Gods. Now it is this Overmind that has up to the present governed our world: it is the highest that man has been able to attain in illumined consciousness. It has been taken for the Supreme Divine and all those who have reached it have never for a moment doubted that they have touched the true Spirit. For, its splendours are so great to the ordinary human consciousness that it is absolutely dazzled into believing that here at last is the crowning reality. And yet the fact is that the Overmind is far below the true Divine. It is not the authentic home of the Truth. It is only the domain of the *formateurs*, all those creative powers and deities to whom men have bowed down since the beginning of history. And the reason why the true Divine has not manifested and transformed the earth-nature is precisely that the Overmind has been mistaken for the Supermind. The cosmic Gods do not wholly live in the Truth-Consciousness: they are only in touch with it and represent, each of them, an aspect of its glories.

No doubt, the Supermind has also acted in the history of the world but always through the Overmind. It is the direct descent of the Supramental Consciousness and Power that alone can utterly re-create life in terms of the Spirit. For, in the Overmind there is already the play of possibilities which marks the beginning of this lower triple world of Mind, Life and Matter in which we have our existence. And whenever there is this play and not the spontaneous and infallible working of the innate Truth of the Spirit, there is the seed of distortion and ignorance. Not that the Overmind is a field of ignorance; but it is the borderline between the Higher and the Lower, for, the play of possibilities, of separate even if not yet divided choice, is likely to lead to deviation from the Truth of things.

The Overmind, therefore, does not and cannot possess the power to transform humanity into divine nature. For that, the Supramental is the sole effective agent.[84]   — THE MOTHER

*

Supermind

> *Here it is written: "It is very unwise for anyone to claim prematurely to have possession of the supermind or even to have a taste of it."* [Sri Aurobindo, *Bases of Yoga*]
> *What is a foretaste of the supermind?*

It is still more unwise to imagine that one has it. That's it.

Yes, because some people, as soon as they find a phrase in a book, in a teaching, immediately imagine that they have realised that. So, when Sri Aurobindo began speaking about the supermind — in what he was writing — everyone wrote to him: "I have seen the supramental Light, I had an experience of the supermind!" Now, it is better to keep the word "supermind" for a later time. For the moment let us not speak about it.

Somewhere he has written a very detailed description of all the mental functions accessible to man. Well, when we read this, we say that merely to traverse the mental domain to its highest limit there are so many stages which have not yet been crossed that truly we don't need to speak about the supermind for the time being.

When he speaks of the higher ranges of the mind, one becomes aware that one very rarely lives in these places. It is very rare for one to be in this state of consciousness. On the contrary it is in what he calls the altogether ordinary mind, the mind of the ordinary man, that we live. And to the ordinary consciousness the reason seems to belong to a very high region; and the reason for him is one of the average faculties of the human mind. There are mental regions very much higher than that, which he has described in detail. And it is quite certain that those correspondents, if they had... Suddenly they said that they were having wonderful supramental experiences, because one is rarely in these regions which lie beyond the reason, which are regions of direct perception, intuition and other faculties of intuition of the same kind, which go far beyond the reason; and these are still mental regions, they have nothing of the supramental.

...it is in the mind itself, without coming out of the mind, that there are all these regions which are almost inaccessible for most human beings.

...Before reaching the extreme limit of the mind, there are so many regions and mental activities which are not at all accessible to most human beings. And even for those who can reach them, they are not regions where they constantly live. They must make an effort of concentration to get there and they don't always arrive. There are regions which Sri Aurobindo has described which only very rare individuals can reach, and still he speaks of them as mental regions. He does not use for them the word supramental.[85]

THE MOTHER

Atman — Self—Spirit

There is no distinction between the Self and the spirit. The psychic is the soul that develops in the evolution — the spirit is the Self that is not affected by the evolution, it is above it — only it is covered or concealed by the activity of mind, vital and the body. The removal of this covering is the release of the spirit — and it is removed when there is a full and wide spiritual silence.[86]   — SRI AUROBINDO

*

When one becomes aware of the Self calm, silent, wide, universal, it is no longer covered over by the ignorance, when one identifies with the Self and not with the mind, life and

body and their movements or with their small ego, that is
the release of the Self.[87]   — SRI AUROBINDO

*

The Atman is the Self or Spirit that remains above, pure and
stainless, unaffected by the stains of life, by desire and ego
and ignorance. It is realised as the true being of the individual, but also more widely as the same being in all and as
the Self in the cosmos; it has also a self-existence above the
individual and cosmos and it is then called the Paramatma,
the supreme Divine Being.[88]   — SRI AUROBINDO

*

The Divine is more than the Atman. It is Nature also. It contains everything in Itself.[89]   — SRI AUROBINDO

Jivatman — Central Being

The self, Atman is in its nature either transcendent or universal (Paramatma, Atma). When it individualises and becomes
a central being, it is then the Jivatman. The Jivatman feels
his oneness with the universal but at the same time his central separateness as a portion of the Divine.[90]

SRI AUROBINDO

*

The phrase "central being" in our yoga is usually applied to the portion of the Divine in us which supports all the rest and survives through death and birth. This central being has two forms — above, it is Jivatman, our true being, of which we become aware when the higher self-knowledge comes, — below, it is the psychic being which stands behind mind, body and life. The Jivatman is above the manifestation in life and presides over it; the psychic being stands behind the manifestation in life and supports it.[91]   — SRI AUROBINDO

*

The central being — the Jivatman which is not born nor evolves but presides over the individual birth and evolution — puts forward a representative of himself on each plane of the consciousness. On the mental plane it is the true mental being, *manomaya puruṣa*, on the vital plane the true vital being, *prāṇamaya puruṣa*, on the physical plane the true physical being, *annamaya puruṣa*. Each being, therefore is, so long as the Ignorance lasts, centred round his mental, vital or physical Purusha, according to the plane on which he predominantly lives, and that is to him his central being. But the true representative all the time is concealed behind the mind, vital and physical — it is the psychic, our inmost being.[92]   — SRI AUROBINDO

*

The true inner being — the true mental, the true vital, the true physical represent each on its plane and answer to the central being, but the whole of the nature and especially the outer nature does not, nor the ordinary mental, vital or physical personality. The psychic being is the central being for the purposes of the evolution — it grows and develops; but there is a central being above of which the mind is not aware, which presides unseen over the existence and of which the psychic being is the representative in the manifested nature. It is what is called the Jivatman.[93]

SRI AUROBINDO

*

The Jivatman is for me the Unborn who presides over the individual being and its developments, associated with it but above it and them and who by the very nature of his existence knows himself as universal and transcendent no less than individual and feels the Divine to be his origin, the truth of his being, the master of his nature, the very stuff of his existence.[94]

— SRI AUROBINDO

*

By Jivatma we mean the individual self. Essentially it is one self with all others, but in the multiplicity of the Divine it is the individual self, an individual centre of the universe — and it sees everything in itself or itself in everything or both together according to its state of consciousness and point of view.[95]

— SRI AUROBINDO

Soul and Psychic Being

The Jivatman, spark-soul and psychic being are three different forms of the same reality and they must not be mixed up together, as that confuses the clearness of the inner experience.

The Jivatman or spirit, as it is usually called in English, is self-existent above the manifested or instrumental being — it is superior to birth and death, always the same, the individual Self or Atman. It is the eternal true being of the individual.

The soul is a spark of the Divine which is not seated above the manifested being, but comes down into the manifestation to support its evolution in the material world. It is at first an undifferentiated power of the Divine Consciousness containing all possibilities which have not yet taken form, but to which it is the function of evolution to give form. This spark is there in all living beings from the lowest to the highest.

The psychic being is formed by the soul in its evolution. It supports the mind, vital, body, grows by their experiences, carries the nature from life to life. It is the psychic or *caitya puruṣa*. At first it is veiled by mind, vital and body, but as it grows, it becomes capable of coming forward and dominating the mind, life and body; in the ordinary man it depends on them for expression and is not able to take them up and freely use them. The life of the being is animal or human and not divine. When the psychic being can by sadhana become dominant and freely use its instruments, then the impulse towards the Divine becomes complete and the transformation of mind, vital and body, not merely their liberation, becomes possible.

The Self or Atman being free and superior to birth and
death, the experience of the Jivatman and its unity with the
supreme or universal Self brings the sense of liberation, it is
this which is necessary for the supreme spiritual deliverance:
but for the transformation of the life and nature the awaken-
ing of the psychic being and its rule over the nature are indispensable.[96]   — SRI AUROBINDO

*

The soul, representative of the central being, is a spark of
the Divine supporting all individual existence in Nature; the
psychic being is a conscious form of that soul growing in
the evolution — in the persistent process that develops first
life in Matter, mind in life, until finally mind can develop
into overmind and overmind into the supramental Truth. The
soul supports the nature in its evolution through these
grades, but is itself not any of these things.[97]

SRI AUROBINDO

*

The psychic being is organised *around* the divine spark. The
divine spark is one, universal, the same everywhere and in
everything, one and infinite, of the same kind in all. You
cannot say that it is a being — it is *the being*, if you like, but
not *a being*. Naturally, if you go back to the origin, you may
say that there is only one soul, for the origin of all souls is
the same, as the origin of the whole universe is the same, as
the origin of the entire creation is the same. But the psychic

being is an individual, personal being with its own experience, its own development, its own growth, its own organisation; only, this organisation is the product of the action of a central divine spark.

But the day an external being (physical, mental, vital) enters into direct and constant contact with the psychic being, one may say in the same way that the *physical* being of this person is organised by the central divine consciousness.[98]

THE MOTHER

*

The soul or psyche is immutable only in the sense that it contains all the possibilities of the Divine within it, but it has to evolve them and in its evolution it assumes the form of a developing psychic individual evolving in the manifestation the individual Prakriti and taking part in the evolution. It is the spark of the Divine Fire that grows behind the mind, vital and physical by means of the psychic being until it is able to transform the Prakriti of Ignorance into a Prakriti of Knowledge. This evolving psychic being is not therefore at any time all that the soul or essential psychic existence bears within it; it temporalises and individualises what is eternal in potentiality, transcendent in essence, in this projection of the spirit.

The central being is the being which presides over the different births one after the other, but is itself unborn, for it does not descend into the being but is above it — it holds together the mental, vital and physical being and all the various parts of the personality and it controls the life either through the mental being and the mental thought and will or through the psychic, whichever may happen to be most in front or most powerful in nature. If it does not exercise its control, then the consciousness is in great disorder and every part of the personality acts for itself so that there is no coherence in the thought, feeling or action.

The psychic is not above but behind — its seat is behind the heart, its power is not knowledge but an essential or spiritual feeling — it has the clearest sense of the Truth and a sort of inherent perception of it which is of the nature of soul-perception and soul-feeling. It is our inmost being and supports all the others, mental, vital, physical, but it is also much veiled by them and has to act upon them as an influence rather than by its sovereign right of direct action; its direct action becomes normal and preponderant only at a high stage of development or by yoga. It is not the psychic being which, you feel, gives you the intuitions of things to be or warns you against the results of certain actions; that is some part of the inner being, sometimes the inner mental, sometimes the inner vital, sometimes, it may be, the inner or subtle physical Purusha. The inner being — inner mind, inner vital, inner or subtle physical — knows much that is unknown to the outer mind, the outer vital, the outer physical, for it is in a more direct contact with the secret forces of Nature. The psychic is the inmost being of all; a perception of truth which is inherent in the deepest substance of the consciousness, a sense of the good, true, beautiful, the Divine, is its privilege.[99]

SRI AUROBINDO

*

The word 'soul', as also the word 'psychic', is used very vaguely and in many different senses in the English language. More often than not, in ordinary parlance, no clear distinction is made between mind and soul and often there is an even more serious confusion, for the vital being of desire — the false soul or desire-soul — is intended by the words 'soul' and 'psychic' and not the true soul, the psychic being. The psychic being is quite different from the mind or vital; it stands behind them where they meet in the heart. Its central place is there, but behind the heart rather than in the heart; for what men call usually the heart is the seat of emotion, and human emotions are mental-vital impulses, not ordinarily psychic in their nature. This mostly secret power behind, other than the mind and the life-force, is the true soul, the psychic being in us. The power of the psychic, however, can act upon the mind and vital and body, purifying thought and perception and emotion (which then becomes psychic feeling) and sensation and action and everything else in us and preparing them to be divine movements.[100]

— SRI AUROBINDO

*

Are the soul and the psychic being one and the same thing?

That depends on the definition you give to the words. In most religions, and perhaps in most philosophies also, it is the vital being which is called "soul", for it is said that "the soul leaves the body", while it is the vital being which leaves the

body. One speaks of "saving the soul", "wicked souls", "redeeming the soul"... but all that applies to the vital being,
for the psychic being has no need to be saved! It does not
share the faults of the external person, it is free from all
reaction.[101]

THE MOTHER

*

The soul or spark is there before the development of an organised vital and mind. The soul is something of the Divine
that descends into the evolution as a divine Principle within
it to support the evolution of the individual out of the Ignorance into the Light. It develops in the course of the evolution a psychic individual or soul individuality which grows
from life to life, using the evolving mind, vital and body as
its instruments. It is the soul that is immortal while the rest
disintegrates; it passes from life to life carrying its experience in essence and the continuity of the evolution of the
individual.[102]   — SRI AUROBINDO

*

*Mother, here Sri Aurobindo speaks of "the psychic
behind supporting all". What does this mean?*

Well, yes, the psychic is behind the whole organisation, this
triple organisation of human life and consciousness, the psychic is behind and supports it by its consciousness which is
an immortal one. It is because of the psychic that we have

so clear a sense of continuity. Otherwise if you compare what you now are with what you were when you were three, obviously you couldn't recognise yourself in any way, either physically or vitally or mentally. There is no resemblance of any kind. But behind there is the psychic which supports the development, the growth of the being and gives this continuity of consciousness, makes one feel that he is the same being even while being absolutely different, absolutely different. If later one observes himself sufficiently, he can see that the things he understood and could do at that time are things which seem to him absolutely inconceivable now, and that he could never do a similar thing because he is no longer that person at all. And yet, because within there was the psychic consciousness which is immortal, one has the feeling that it is always the same being which was there and continues to be there and will continue to be there with more or less progressive and more or less conscious changes.[103]   — THE MOTHER

*

A distinction has to be made between the soul in its essence and the psychic being. Behind each and all there is the soul which is the spark of the Divine — none could exist without that. But it is quite possible to have a vital and physical being without a clearly evolved psychic being behind it....

The inner being is composed of the inner mental, inner vital, inner physical, — but that is not the psychic being. The psychic is the inmost being and quite distinct from these. The word 'psychic' is indeed used in English to indicate any-

thing that is other or deeper than the external mind, life and
body, anything occult or supraphysical, but that is a use which
brings confusion and error and we entirely discard it....

The psychic being is veiled by the surface movements and
expresses itself as best it can through these outer instruments
which are more governed by the outer forces than by the
inner influences of the psychic. But that does not mean that
they are entirely isolated from the soul. The soul is in the
body in the same way as the mind or vital — but the body it
occupies is not this gross physical frame only, but the subtle
body also. When the gross sheath falls away, the vital and
mental sheaths of the body still remain as the soul's vehicle
till these too dissolve.[104]   — SRI AUROBINDO

*

*Sweet Mother, can the psychic express itself without
the mind, the vital and the physical?*

It expresses itself constantly without them. Only, in order
that the ordinary human being may perceive it, it has to express itself through them, because the ordinary human being is not in direct contact with the psychic. If it was in
direct contact with the psychic it would be psychic in its
manifestation — and all would be truly well. But as it is not
in contact with the psychic it doesn't even know what it is, it
wonders all bewildered what kind of a being it can be; so to
reach this ordinary human consciousness it must use ordinary means, that is, go through the mind, the vital and the
physical.

One of them may be skipped but surely not the last, otherwise one is no longer conscious of anything at all.[105]

THE MOTHER

*

The soul and the life are two quite different powers. The soul is a spark of the Divine Spirit which supports the individual nature; mind, life, body are the instruments for the manifestation of the nature. In most men the soul is hidden and covered over by the action of the external nature; they mistake the vital being for the soul, because it is the vital which animates and moves the body. But this vital being is a thing made up of desires and executive forces, good and bad; it is the desire-soul, not the true thing. It is when the true soul (psyche) comes forward and begins first to influence and then govern the actions of the instrumental nature that man begins to overcome vital desire and grow towards a divine nature.[106] — SRI AUROBINDO

*

Sweet Mother, here Sri Aurobindo has said: "If the inmost soul is awakened, if there is a new birth out of the mere mental, vital and physical into the psychic consciousness, then this Yoga can be done..." Why has he said "the inmost soul"? Is there a superficial soul?

It is because this inmost soul, that is, the central psychic being, influences the superficial parts of the consciousness (superficial in comparison with it: mental parts, vital parts). The purest mind, the highest vital, the emotive being — the soul influences them, influences them to an extent where one has the impression of entering into contact with it through these parts of the being. So people take these parts for the soul and that is why he says "the inmost soul", that is, the central soul, the real soul.

For very often, when one touches certain parts of the mind which are under the psychic influence and full of light and the joy of that light, or when one touches certain very pure and very high parts of the emotive being which has the most generous, most unselfish emotions, one also has the impression of being in contact with one's soul. But this is not the true soul, it is not the soul in its very essence. These are parts of the being under its influence and manifesting something of it. So, very often people enter into contact with these parts and this gives them illuminations, great joy, revelations, and they feel they have found their soul. But it is only the part of the being under its influence, one part or another.... Exactly what happens is that one touches these things, has experiences, and then it gets veiled, and one wonders, "How is it that I touched my soul and now have fallen back into this state of ignorance and inconscience!" But that's because one had not touched one's soul, one had touched those parts of the being which are under the influence of the soul and manifest something of it, but are not it.

I have already said many times that when one enters consciously into contact with one's soul and the union is established, it is over, it can no longer be undone, it is something permanent, constant, which resists everything, and which, at any moment whatever, if referred to can be found; whereas the other things — one can have very fine experiences, and then it gets veiled again, and one tells oneself, "How does that happen? I saw my soul and now I don't find it any more!" It was not the soul one had seen. And these things are very beautiful and give you very impressive experiences, but this is not the contact with the psychic being itself.

The contact with the psychic being is definitive, and it is about this that I say, when people ask, "Do I have a contact with my psychic being?", "Your question itself proves that you don't have it!"[107]   — THE MOTHER

*

... you must not mistake the feelings for the psychic, you understand! — these two are absolutely different things. People always think that when they have emotions, feelings, they are entering the psychic. These things have nothing to do with the psychic, they are purely vital. They are the most subtle part of the vital, if you like, but they are vital. It's not through the feelings that one goes to the psychic, it is through a very intense aspiration and a self-detachment.[108]

THE MOTHER

*

The soul is that which comes out of the Divine without ever leaving Him and goes back to Him without ever ceasing from manifestation.

The soul is the Divine made individual without ceasing to

be divine. In the soul the individual and the Divine are eternally one.

Thus to find one's soul is to be united with the Divine.

It can therefore be said that the role of the soul is to make of man a true being.[109]   — THE MOTHER

*

... if there were no psychic in Matter, it would not be able to have any direct contact with the Divine. And it is happily due to this psychic presence in Matter that the contact between Matter and the Divine can be direct and all human beings can be told, "You carry the Divine within you, and you have only to enter within yourself and you will find Him." It is something very particular to the human being or rather to the inhabitants of the earth. In the human being the psychic becomes more conscious, more formed, more conscious and more independent also. It is individualised in human beings. But it is a speciality of the earth. It is a direct infusion, special and redeeming, in the most inconscient and obscure Matter, so that it might once again awake through stages to the divine Consciousness, the divine Presence and finally to the Divine Himself. It is the presence of the psychic which makes man an exceptional being — I don't like to tell him this very much, because already he thinks too much of himself; he has such a high opinion of himself that it is not necessary to encourage him! But still, this is a fact — so much so that there are beings of other domains of the universe, those called by some people demigods and even gods, beings, for instance, of what Sri Aurobindo calls the

Overmind, who are very eager to take a physical body on earth to have the experience of the psychic, for they don't have it. These beings certainly have many qualities that men don't, but they lack this divine presence which is altogether exceptional and exists only on the earth and nowhere else. All these inhabitants of the higher worlds, the Higher Mind, Overmind and other regions have no psychic being. Of course, the beings of the vital worlds don't have it either. But these latter don't regret it, they don't want it. There are only those very rare ones, quite exceptional, who want to be converted, and for this they act without delay, they immediately take a physical body. The others don't want it; it is something which binds them and constrains them to a rule they do not want.

But it is a fact, so I am obliged to state that this is how it is, that it is an exceptional quality of the human being to carry within himself the psychic and, truly speaking, he does not take full advantage from it. He does not seem to consider this quality as something very, very desirable, from the way he treats this presence — exactly that! He prefers to it the ideas of his mind, prefers the desires of his vital being and the habits of his physical.[110]   — THE MOTHER

*

Mother, does an individual's life depend on the experience his psychic being wants to have?

Very much!

I was speaking about just this with someone today, and I

said this, that if one can become fully conscious of his psychic being, at the same time one understands, necessarily, the reason of his present existence and the experience this psychic being wants to have; and instead of having it somewhat half-consciously and more than half unconsciously, one can shorten this experience and so help his psychic being to cover in a limited number of years the experiences it would perhaps take several lifetimes to go through. That is to say, the help is reciprocal. The psychic, when it has an influence on the outer life, brings to it light, order and quietude and the joy of the divine contact. But also the physical being, the body-consciousness, if it is identified with the psychic consciousness, and through that learns what kind of experience the psychic being wants to have, it can help it to have these experiences in a very brief time, and not only save time but save many lives for the psychic being. It is a mutual help.

In brief, this is what yoga means. Yoga helps you to become fully conscious of your destiny, that is, your mission in the universe, and not only at the present moment but what it was in the past and what it will be in the future. And because of this knowledge you can gather by a concentration of the consciousness all these experiences in a very short time and gain lives, do in a few years what could take a fairly considerable number of lives to achieve. The psychic being goes progressively through all these experiences towards its full maturity and complete independence, its liberation — in the sense that it no longer needs any new life. If it wants to come back to the physical world, it returns, because it has something to do there and it chooses freely to return. But till then, till this liberation, it is compelled to return to have all the experiences it needs. Well, if it happens that once the physical being is developed and conscious enough and has enough goodwill to be able to become fully aware of the psychic being, it can then and there create all the circumstances, the outer experiences necessary for the psychic being to attain its maturity in this very life.[111]   — THE MOTHER

*

Sweet Mother, is identification with the psychic the same thing as the psychic coming in front?

That is, the first step is the identification, and then, once you can keep this identification, the psychic governs the rest of the nature and life. It becomes the master of existence. So this is what we mean by the psychic coming in front. It is that which governs, directs, even organises the life, organises the consciousness, the different parts of the being. When this happens, the work goes very fast. Very fast, well... relatively very fast.

In the human consciousness everything is *very slow*. When we compare the time that is necessary to realise something with the average length of human existence, it seems interminable. But happily there comes a time when one escapes from this notion, when one begins to feel no longer according to human measures. As soon as one is truly in touch with the psychic, one loses this kind of narrowness and of agony also, this agony which is so bad: "I must be quick, I must be quick, there is not much time, I must hurry, there is not much time." One does things very badly or doesn't do them at all any more. But as soon as there is a contact with the psychic, then indeed this disappears; one begins to be a little more vast and calm and peaceful, and to live in eternity.[112]

THE MOTHER

*

What is meant by [the psychic's] coming to the front is simply this. The psychic ordinarily is deep within. Very few people are aware of their souls — when they speak of their soul, they usually mean the vital + mental being or else the (false) soul of desire. The psychic remains behind and acts only through the mind, vital and physical wherever it can. For this reason the psychic being except where it is very much developed has only a small and partial, concealed and mixed or diluted influence on the life of most men. By coming forward is meant that it comes from behind the veil, its presence is felt already in the waking daily consciousness, its influence fills, dominates, transforms the mind and vital and their movements, even the physical. One is aware of one's soul, feels the psychic to be one's true being, the mind and the rest begin to be only instruments of the inmost within us.

The inner mental, vital, physical are also veiled, but much nearer to the surface and much of their movements or inspirations get through the veil (but not in any fullness or purity) in the lives of developed human beings, something even in the lives of ordinary people. But these too in yoga throw down the veil after a time and come in front and their action predominates in the consciousness while the external is no longer felt as one's own self but only as a front or even a fringe of the being.[113]   — SRI AUROBINDO

*

> "The nexus between the psychic being and the higher consciousness is the principal means of the siddhi."
>
> Sri Aurobindo, *Lights on Yoga*

Ordinarily is there not a nexus between the psychic being and the higher consciousness?

Ordinarily means in the ordinary life? A relation between the psychic being...

Yes.

It is almost, almost totally unconscious.

In the ordinary life there's not one person in a million who has a conscious contact with his psychic being, even momentarily. The psychic being may work from within, but so invisibly and unconsciously for the outer being that it is as though it did not exist. And in most cases, the immense majority, almost the totality of cases, it's as though it were asleep, not at all active, in a kind of torpor.

It is only with the sadhana and a very persistent effort that one succeeds in having a conscious contact with his psychic being. Naturally, it is possible that there are exceptional cases — but this is truly exceptional, and they are so few that they could be counted — where the psychic being is an entirely formed, liberated being, master of itself, which has chosen to return to earth in a human body in order to do its work. And in this case, even if the person doesn't do the sadhana consciously, it is possible that the psychic being is powerful enough to establish a more or less conscious relation. But these cases are, so to say, unique and are exceptions which confirm the rule.

In almost, almost all cases, a very, very sustained effort is needed to become aware of one's psychic being. Usually it is considered that if one can do it in thirty years one is very lucky — thirty years of sustained effort, I say. It may happen that it's quicker. But this is so rare that immediately one says, "This is not an ordinary human being." That's the case of people who have been considered more or less divine beings and who were great yogis, great initiates.[114]

THE MOTHER

True Being and Ego

The true being may be realised in one or both of two aspects — the Self or Atman and the soul or Antaratman, psychic being, Chaitya Purusha. The difference is that one is felt as universal, the other as individual supporting the mind, life and body. When one first realises the Atman one feels it separate from all things, existing in itself and detached, and it is to this realisation that the image of the dry coconut fruit may apply. When one realises the psychic being, it is not like that; for this brings the sense of union with the Divine and dependence upon It and sole consecration to the Divine alone and the power to change the nature and discover the true mental, the true vital, the true physical being in oneself. Both realisations are necessary for this yoga.

The "I" or the little ego is constituted by Nature and is at once a mental, vital and physical formation meant to aid in centralising and individualising the outer consciousness and action. When the true being is discovered, the utility of the ego is over and this formation has to disappear — the true being is felt in its place.[115]   — SRI AUROBINDO

*

... man is not aware of the self or Jivatman, he is aware only of his ego, or he is aware of the mental being which controls the life and the body. But more deeply he becomes aware of his soul or psychic being as his true centre, the Purusha in the heart; the psychic is the central being in the evolution, it proceeds from and represents the Jivatman, the eternal portion of the Divine. When there is the full consciousness, the Jivatman and the psychic being join together.

The ego is a formation of Nature; but it is not a formation of physical nature alone, therefore it does not cease with the body. There is a mental and vital ego also.[116]

SRI AUROBINDO

*

In a certain sense the various Purushas or beings in us, psychic, mental, vital, physical are projections of the Atman, but that gets its full truth only when we get into our inner being and know the inner truth of ourselves. On the surface, in the Ignorance, it is the mental, vital, physical Prakriti that acts and the Purusha is disfigured, as it were, in the action of the Prakriti. It is not our true mental being, our true vital being, our true physical being even that we are aware of; these remain behind, veiled and silent. It is the mental, vital, physical ego that we take for our being until we get knowledge.[117]   — SRI AUROBINDO

*

The true being mental, vital or subtle physical has always the greater qualities of its plane — it is the Purusha and like the psychic, though in another way, the projection of the Divine, therefore in connection with the higher consciousness and reflects something of it, though it is not altogether that — it is also in tune with the cosmic Truth.

There is behind all the vital nature in man his true vital being concealed and immobile which is quite different from the surface vital nature. The surface vital is narrow, ignorant, limited, full of obscure desires, passions, cravings, revolts, pleasures and pains, transient joys and griefs, exultations and depressions. The true vital being, on the contrary, is wide, vast, calm, strong, without limitations, firm and immovable, capable of all power, all knowledge, all Ananda. It is moreover without ego, for it knows itself to be a projection and instrument of the Divine: it is the divine Warrior, pure and perfect; in it is an instrumental Force for all divine realisations. It is the true vital being that has become awake and come in front within you. In the same way there is too a true mental being, a true physical being. When these are manifest, then you are aware of a double existence in you: that behind is always calm and strong, that on the surface alone is troubled and obscure. But if the true being behind remains stable and you live in it, then the trouble and obscurity remain only on the surface; in this condition the exterior parts can be dealt with more potently and they also made free and perfect.[118]   — SRI AUROBINDO

3

BECOMING AN INDIVIDUAL

Mother, you said one day that before being able to identify oneself with the Divine, one must first become an individual.

Yes, well, that's it, exactly. You are in the period of becoming an individual. And so long as one is in this period of becoming an individual, well, one must wait until this period passes, that is, till you have become a conscious individual. Perfectly. It is that.

Mother, you said there are very few, one in a million perhaps, who are really conscious.

Oh, if you take humanity at large, certainly! And the great mass of mankind will never become individuals, it will always be an amorphous mass, all intermingled, like that (*gesture*). To become an individual is what Sri Aurobindo calls becoming truly a mental man. Well, if you have read *The Human Cycle*, you will see that already it is not so easy to become a truly mental man who thinks by himself, is free from all outer influences, who has an individuality, who exists, has his reality; even that is not so easy.

But, by a kind of Grace, it can happen that before becoming an individual, if someone has within himself an aspiration, if he feels the need to awaken to something which would want more, want something better, which feels how very small it is to be an individual, something which really seeks beyond the ordinary limits, well, even before becoming an individual, he may suddenly have the experience of a contact with his psychic which opens all the doors for him. They close again later, but once they have opened you never forget it. The remembrance remains very vividly....[119] — THE MOTHER

*

Sweet Mother, why are we so attached to our ego?

As I said just now, probably because you still need it very much, isn't that so? In order to become a conscious, individualised being, one needs his ego; that is why it is there. It is only when one has realised his own individuality sufficiently, has become a conscious, independent being with its own reality, that he no longer needs the ego. And at that time one can make an effort to get rid of it. Unfortunately most people, as soon as they become real individuals, have such a sense of their importance and their ability that they no longer even think at all of getting rid of their ego. But that of course is something else.

Here I don't let you go to sleep. I remind you from time to time of the true thing. But you are all very young, you see, and a certain number of years are *needed*, years of intensive inner formation, to become a being who thinks for himself, is conscious of his own will, and conscious of his own nature, his purpose of existence, independent of the human mass. A certain time is necessary. Some children begin when *very small*. If one begins very early, when one is twenty he can be quite formed. But you must begin when very small, and consciously, very consciously; you must begin with a sense of observation of all the movements in yourself, of their relation with others, of — precisely, of your degree of independence, real individuality, of knowing where impulses come from, where other movements come from: whether it is contagion from outside or something that arises from within yourself. A very profound study of all the movements in oneself is necessary in order to succeed simply in crystallising a being who is a little conscious, *a little* conscious. But when you live fluidly, so to say, when you don't even know what goes on inside you, have some sort of vague impressions, if you question yourself, at least ninety-nine times out of a hundred, if you ask yourself, "Why did I think like that? Why did I feel like that?", even "Why did I do that?", then the reply is almost always the same: "I don't know. It came like that, that's all." That is to say, one is not at all conscious.

Are you able to know, when you are with others, what comes from you and what from the others? To what extent their way of being, their particular vibrations act upon you? You are not aware of this at all. You live in a kind of "approximate" consciousness, half-awake, half-asleep, in something very vague, where you have to grope like this in order to catch things. But do you have a precise, clear, exact notion of what goes on in you, why it goes on in you? And then, this: the vibrations which come to you from outside and those which come from within you? And then, again, what can come from others, changing all this, giving another orientation? You live in a kind of hazy fluidity, certain small things suddenly crystallise in your consciousness, you have just caught them for a moment; and it is just clear enough like that, as though there was a projector, just something passing on the screen and becoming clear for a second: the next minute everything has become vague, imprecise, but you are not aware of this because you have not even asked yourself the question, because you live in this way. It stops here, begins here, ends here. That's all. You do from day to day, minute to minute, things which you do, like that... it happens to be like that.[120]

THE MOTHER

*

Ego means what?

I think it is the ego that makes each one a separate being, in all possible ways. It is the ego which gives the sense of being a person separate from others. It is certainly the ego which gives you the sense of the "I", "I am", "I want", "I do", "I exist", even the very famous "I think therefore I am" which is... I am sorry but I think it is a stupidity — but still it is a celebrated stupidity — well, this too is the ego. What gives you the impression that you are Manoj is the ego, and that you are altogether different from this one and that one; and what prevents your body from melting away like that, dissolving in a common mass of physical vibrations, is the ego; what gives you a definite form, a definite character, a separate consciousness, the sense that you exist in yourself, independently of all others, indeed, something like that; if one does not reflect, spontaneously one has the sense that even if the world disappeared, one would be there, one would remain what one is. This of course is the super-ego.

Certainly, if one were to lose one's ego too soon, from the vital and mental point of view one would again become an amorphous mass. The ego is surely the instrument for individualisation, that is, until one is an individualised being, constituted in himself, the ego is an absolutely necessary factor. If one had the power of abolishing the ego ahead of time, one would lose one's individuality. But once the individuality has been formed, the ego becomes not only useless but harmful. And only then comes the time when it must be abolished. But naturally, as it has taken so much trouble to build you, it does not give up its work so easily, and it asks for the reward of its efforts, that is, to enjoy the individuality.[121]

THE MOTHER

*

So there is a long, long, long way to go before merging one's ego in the Divine.

Merge one's ego in the Divine! But first, one can't merge one's ego in the Divine before becoming completely individualised. Do you know what it means to be *completely* individualised? Capable of resisting all outer influences?

Some days ago I received a letter from someone who told me that he was very hesitant about reading books of ordinary literature, for example, novels or dramas, because his nature had an almost insuperable tendency to receive imprints of the characters in these books and to begin living the feelings and thoughts of these characters, the nature of these persons. There are many more people than one would think who are like that.

They read a book and while they are reading it they feel within themselves all kinds of emotions, thoughts, desires, intentions, plans, even ideals. They are simply just absorbed in the reading of the book. They are not even aware of it, because at least ninety-nine parts of an individual's character are made of soft butter — inedible of course... but on which if one presses one's thumb, an imprint is made.

Now, everything is a "thumb": an expressed thought, a sentence read, an object looked at, an observation of what someone else does, and of one's neighbour's will. And all these wills... you know, when one sees them they are all there, like this, intermingled (*Mother intercrosses her fingers*), each one trying to get the uppermost and causing a kind of perpetual conflict within, outside.... It goes in and out of people like that, you see, like electric currents. One is not at all aware of all this, and it is a perpetual conflict of all the wills which are trying to express themselves; and the strongest one will succeed. But as there are many of these and as one has to fight alone against a great number, it is not easy.

So one is tossed like a cork on the waves of the sea.... One day one wants this, the next day one wants that, at one moment one is pushed from this side, at another from that, now one lifts one's face to the sky (*Mother makes the movement*), now one is sunk deep in a hole. And so this is the existence one has!

First one must become a conscious, well-knit, *individualised* being, who exists in himself, by himself, independently of all his surroundings, who can hear anything, read anything, see anything without changing. He receives from outside only what he wants to receive; he automatically refuses all that is not in conformity with his plan and nothing can leave an imprint on him unless he agrees to receive the imprint. Then one begins to become an individuality! When one is an individuality, one can make an offering of it.

For, unless one possesses something, one cannot give it. First, one must be, and then afterwards one can give oneself.

So long as one does not exist, one can give nothing. And for the separative ego to disappear, as you say, one must be able to give oneself entirely, totally without reservation. And to be able to give oneself, one must first exist. And to exist one must be individualised.

If your body were not made in the rigid form it is – for it is terribly rigid, isn't it? — well, if all that were not so fixed, if you had no skin, here, like this, solid, if externally you were the reflection of what you are in the vital and mental fields, it would be worse than being a jelly-fish! Everything would fuse into everything else, like this…. Oh, what a mess it would be! That is why it was at first necessary to give a very rigid form. Afterwards we complain about it. We say, "The physical is fixed, it is a nuisance; it lacks plasticity, it lacks suppleness, it hasn't that fluidity which can enable us to merge into the Divine." But this was absolutely necessary, for without this… if you simply went out of your body (most of you can't do it because the vital being is hardly more individualised than the physical), if you came out of your body and went into the vital world, you would see that all things there intermingle, they are mixed, they divide; all kinds of vibrations, currents of forces come and go, struggle, try to destroy one another, take possession of each other, absorb each other, throw each other out… and so it goes on! But it is very difficult to find a real personality in all this. These are forces, movements, desires, vibrations.

There are individualities, there are personalities! But these are powers. People who are individualised in that world are either heroes or devils!

And now, in the mind... (*Silence*) If only you become conscious of your physical mind in itself... Some people have called it a public square, because everything comes there, goes across, passes, comes back.... All ideas go there, they enter at one place, leave by another, some are here, some there, and it is a public square, not very well organised, for usually ideas meet and knock into one another, there are accidents of all kinds. But then one becomes aware: "*What can I call my mind?*" or "*What is my mind?*"

One needs years of very attentive, very careful, very reasonable, very coherent work, organisation, selection, construction, in order to succeed simply in forming, oh, simply this little thing, *one's own way of thinking!*

One believes he has his own way of thinking. Not at all. It depends totally upon the people one speaks with or the books he has read or on the mood he is in. It depends also on whether you have a good or bad digestion, it depends on whether you are shut up in a room without proper ventilation or whether you are in the open air; it depends on whether you have a beautiful landscape before you; it depends on whether there is sunshine or rain! You are not aware of it, but you think all kinds of things, completely different according to a heap of things which have nothing to do with you!

And for this to become a coordinated, coherent, logical thought, a long, thorough work is necessary. And then, the best of the business is that when you have succeeded in making a beautiful, well-formed, very strong, very powerful mental construction, the first thing you will be told is, "You must break this so that you can unite with the Divine!" But so long as you haven't made it, you cannot unite with the Divine because you have nothing to give to the Divine except a mass of things which are not yourself! *One must first exist in order to be able to give oneself.* I am repeating what I said a while ago.[122]

　　　　　　　　　　　　　　　　　　　— THE MOTHER

*

All this... it is not in order to swamp you that I tell you all this. It is only in order to tell you that before speaking of merging one's ego in the Divine, one must first know a little what one is. The ego is there. Its necessity is that you become conscious, independent beings, individualised – I mean in the sense of independent – that you may not be the public square where every thing goes criss-cross! That you may exist in yourselves. That is why there is an ego. It is like that; that is why also there is a skin, like that... though truly, even physical forces pass through the skin. There is a vibration which goes a certain distance. But still, it's the skin that prevents us from blending into one another. But everything else must be like that too.

　　(*After a silence*) And then, later, one offers all this to the Divine. Years of work are needed. You must not only... (*silence*) ... become conscious of yourself, conscious in all details, but you must organise what you call "yourself" around the psychic centre, the divine centre of your being, so that it would make a single, coherent, fully conscious being. And as this divine centre is itself already consecrated (*Mother makes a gesture of offering*) entirely to the Divine, if everything is organised harmoniously around it, everything is consecrated to the Divine. And so, when the Divine thinks it proper, when the time has come, when the work of individualisation is complete, then the Divine gives you permission to let your ego merge in Him, to live henceforward only for the Divine.

But it is the Divine who takes this decision. You must first have done all this work, become a conscious being, solely and exclusively centred around the Divine and governed by Him. And after all that, there is still an ego; because it is the ego which serves to make you an individual. But once this work is perfect, fully accomplished, then, at that moment, you may tell the Divine, "Here I am, I am ready. Do you want me?" And the Divine usually says, "Yes." All is over, everything is accomplished. And you become a real instrument for the Divine's work. But first the instrument must be constructed.[123]   — THE MOTHER

*

Sweet Mother, when does the ego become an instrument?

When it is ready to become it.

How does that happen?

How does it happen?... In each one, I believe, it happens in a different way. It may happen suddenly, in the space of a moment, by a kind of inner reversal; it may take years; it may take centuries; it may take several lives. For each one there is a moment when it happens: when he is ready.

And I think he is ready when he is completely formed. The purpose of existence of the ego is the formation of the individual. When the individual is ready the ego can disappear. But before that it does not disappear because it has still some work to do.[124]   — THE MOTHER

4

BECOMING CONSCIOUS

To become conscious of what is to be changed in the nature is the first step towards changing it. But one must observe these things without being despondent or thinking "it is hopeless" or "I cannot change".[125] — SRI AUROBINDO

*

"To know oneself and control oneself". — The Mother

What does this mean?

This means to be conscious of one's inner truth, conscious of the different parts of one's being and their respective functions. You must know why you do this, why you do that; you must know your thoughts, know your feelings, all your activities, all your movements, of what you are capable, etc. And to know oneself is not enough: this knowledge must bring a conscious control. To know oneself perfectly is to control oneself perfectly.

But there must be an aspiration at every moment.

It is never too early to begin, never too late to continue. That is, even when you are quite young, you can begin to study yourself and know yourself and gradually to control yourself. And even when you are what is called "old", when you are quite aged, it is not too late to make the effort to know yourself better and better and control yourself better and better. That is the Science of Living.

To perfect oneself, one must first become conscious of oneself. I am sure, for instance, that the following situation has arisen many times in your life: someone asks you suddenly, "Why have you done that?" Well, the spontaneous reply is, "I don't know." If someone asks you, "What are you thinking of?" You reply, "I don't know." "Why are you tired?" — "I don't know." "Why are you happy?" — "I don't know", and so on. I can take indeed fifty people and ask them suddenly, without preparation, "Why have you done that?" and if they are not inwardly "awake", they will all answer, "I don't know" (of course I am not speaking here of those who have practised a discipline of self-knowledge and of following up their movements to the extreme limits; these people can, naturally, collect themselves, concentrate and give the right answer, but only after a little while). You will see that it is like that if you look well at your whole day. You say something and you don't know why you say it — it is only after the words are out of your mouth that you notice that this was not quite what you wanted to say. For instance, you go to see someone, you prepare beforehand the words you are going to speak, but once you are in front of the person in question, you say nothing or it is other words which come from your mouth. Are you able to say to what extent the atmosphere of the other person has influenced you and stopped you from saying what you had prepared? How many people can say that? They do not even observe that the person was in such or such a state and that it was because of this that they could not tell him what they had prepared. Of course, there are very obvious instances when you find people in such a bad mood that you can ask nothing of them. I am not speaking of these. I am speaking of the clear perception of reciprocal influences: what acts and reacts on your nature; it is this one does not have. For example, one becomes suddenly uneasy or happy, but how many people can say, "It is this"? And it is difficult to know, it is not at all easy. One must be quite "awake"; one must be constantly in a very attentive state of observation.

There are people who sleep twelve hours a day and say the rest of the time, "I am awake"! There are people who sleep twenty hours a day and the rest of the time are but half awake!

To be in this state of attentive observation, you must have, so to say, antennae everywhere which are in constant contact with your true centre of consciousness. You register everything, you organise everything and, in this way, you cannot be taken unawares, you cannot be deceived, mistaken, and you cannot say anything other than what you wanted to say. But how many people normally live in this state? It is this I mean, precisely, when I speak of "becoming conscious". If you want to benefit most from the conditions and circumstances in which you find yourself, you must be fully awake: you must not be taken by surprise, you must not do things without knowing why, you must not say things without knowing why. You must be constantly awake.

You must also understand that you are not separate individualities, that life is a constant exchange of forces, of consciousnesses, of vibrations, of movements of all kinds. It is as in a crowd, you see: when everyone pushes all go forward, and when all recede, everyone recedes. It is the same thing in the inner world, in your consciousness. There are all the time forces and influences acting and reacting upon you, it is like a gas in the atmosphere, and unless you are quite awake, these things enter into you, and it is only when they have gone well in and come out as if they came from you, that you become aware of them. How many times people meet those who are nervous, angry, in a bad mood, and themselves become nervous, angry, moody, just like that, without quite knowing why. Why is it that when you play against certain people you play very well, but when you play against others you cannot play? And those very quiet people, not at all wicked, who suddenly become furious when they are in a furious crowd! And no one knows who has started it: it is something that went past and swept off the consciousness. There are people who can let out vibrations like this and others respond without knowing why. Everything is like that, from the smallest to the biggest things.

To be individualised in a collectivity, one must be absolutely conscious of oneself. And of which self? — the Self which is above all intermixture, that is, what I call the Truth of your being. And as long as you are not conscious of the Truth of your being, you are moved by all kinds of things, without taking any note of it at all. Collective thought, collective suggestions are a formidable influence which act constantly on individual thought. And what is extraordinary is that one does not notice it. One believes that one thinks "like that", but in truth it is the collectivity which thinks "like that". The mass is always inferior to the individual. Take individuals with similar qualities, of similar categories, well, when they are alone these individuals are at least two degrees better than people of the same category in a crowd. There is a mixture of obscurities, a mixture of unconsciousness, and inevitably you slip into this unconsciousness. To escape this there is but one means: to become conscious of oneself, more and more conscious and more and more attentive.

Try this little exercise: at the beginning of the day, say: "I won't speak without thinking of what I say." You believe, don't you, that you think all that you say! It is not at all true, you will see that so many times the word you do not want to say is ready to come out, and that you are compelled to make a conscious effort to stop it from coming out.

I have known people who were very scrupulous about not telling lies, but all of a sudden, when together in a group, instead of speaking the truth they would spontaneously tell a lie; they did not have the intention of doing so, they did not think of it a minute before doing it, but it came "like that". Why? — because they were in the company of liars; there was an atmosphere of falsehood and they had quite simply caught the malady!

It is thus that gradually, slowly, with perseverance, first of all with great care and much attention, one becomes conscious, learns to know oneself and then to become master of oneself.[126]
                                                        — THE MOTHER

*

What is one to do to prepare oneself for the Yoga?

To be conscious, first of all. We are conscious of only an insignificant portion of our being; for the most part we are unconscious. It is this unconsciousness that keeps us down

to our unregenerate nature and prevents change and transformation in it. It is through unconsciousness that the
undivine forces enter into us and make us their slaves. You
are to be conscious of yourself, you must awake to your
nature and movements, you must know why and how you
do things or feel or think them; you must understand your
motives and impulses, the forces, hidden and apparent, that
move you; in fact, you must, as it were, take to pieces the
entire machinery of your being. Once you are conscious, it
means that you can distinguish and sift things, you can see
which are the forces that pull you down and which help you
on. And when you know the right from the wrong, the true
from the false, the divine from the undivine, you are to act
strictly up to your knowledge; that is to say, resolutely reject one and accept the other. The duality will present itself
at every step and at every step you will have to make your
choice. You will have to be patient and persistent and vigilant—"sleepless", as the adepts say; you must always refuse to give any chance whatever to the undivine against the
divine.[127]   — THE MOTHER

*

... in order to reject anything from the being one has first to
become conscious of it, to have the clear inner experience
of its action and to discover its actual place in the workings
of the nature. One can then work upon it to eliminate it, if it
is an entirely wrong movement, or to transform it if it is
only the degradation of a higher and true movement. It is
this or something like it that is attempted crudely and im-

properly with a rudimentary and insufficient knowledge in the system of psycho-analysis. The process of raising up the lower movements into the full light of consciousness in order to know and deal with them is inevitable; for there can be no complete change without it. But it can truly succeed only when a higher light and force are sufficiently at work to overcome, sooner or later, the force of the tendency that is held up for change.[128] — SRI AUROBINDO

*

To work for your perfection, the first step is to become conscious of yourself, of the different parts of your being and their respective activities. You must learn to distinguish these different parts one from another, so that you may become clearly aware of the origin of the movements that occur in you, the many impulses, reactions and conflicting wills that drive you to action. It is an assiduous study which demands much perseverance and sincerity. For man's nature, especially his mental nature, has a spontaneous tendency to give a favourable explanation for everything he thinks, feels, says and does. It is only by observing these movements with great care, by bringing them, as it were, before the tribunal of our highest ideal, with a sincere will to submit to its judgment, that we can hope to form in ourselves a discernment that never errs. For if we truly want to progress and acquire the capacity of knowing the truth of our being, that is to say, what we are truly created for, what we can call our mission upon earth, then we must, in a very regular and constant manner, reject from us or eliminate in us whatever contradicts the truth of our existence, whatever is opposed to it. In this way, little by little, all the parts, all the elements of our being can be organised into a homogeneous whole around our psychic centre. This work of unification requires much time to be brought to some degree of perfection. Therefore, in order to accomplish it, we must arm ourselves with patience and endurance, with a determination to prolong our life as long as necessary for the success of our endeavour.[129]

— THE MOTHER

*

One must never neglect to clean one's room, it is very important; inner cleanliness is at least as important as outer cleanliness.

Vivekananda has written (I don't know the original, I have only read the French translation): "One must every morning clean one's soul and one's body, but if you don't have time for both, it is better to clean the soul than clean the body."

> *How can one know whether the little dirty things have hidden themselves or have gone?*

One can always try little experiments. I have said that one must use a torch, a strong light; then one must take a round within one's being. If one is very attentive, one can very easily find these ugly corners. Suppose you have a beautiful experience, that suddenly in answer to your aspiration a great light comes; your feel all flooded with joy, force, light, beauty, and have the impression that you are on the point of being transfigured... and then, it passes away — it always passes away, doesn't it? especially at the beginning — suddenly, it stops. Then you tell yourself, when you are not vigilant, "There, it came and it has gone! Poor me! it came and has gone, it just gave me a taste of the thing and then let me fall." Well, that's foolish. What you should tell yourself is, "Look, I was not able to keep it, and why was I not able to keep it?" So, you take your torch and go on a round within yourself trying to find a very close relation between the change of consciousness and the movements accompanying the cessation of the experience. And if you are very, very attentive, and make your round very scrupulously, you will find that suddenly some part of the vital or some part of the mind or of the body, something has not kept up, in this sense that mentally, instead of being immobile and attentive, something has begun to ask, "Wait a minute, what is this experience? What does it mean?", begun to try to find an explanation (what it calls an "understanding"). Or maybe in the vital something has begun to enjoy the experience: "How pleasant it is, how I would like it to grow, how good if it were constant, how..." Or something in the physical has said, "Oh! it is a bit hard to endure that, how long am I going to be able to keep it?" It is perhaps not as obvious as all this, but it is a wee bit hidden like this, somewhere. You will always find one of these three things or others analogous. Then, it is there the lantern is needed: where is the weak point? where is the egoism? where is the desire? where is that old dirt we do not want any longer? where is that thing which turns back upon itself instead of giving itself, opening itself, losing itself? which turns back upon itself, tries to

take advantage of what has happened, wants to appropriate
to itself the fruit of the experience? Or rather which is too
weak, too hard, too rigid to be able to follow the movement?... It is that, you are now on the track, you begin precisely to put the light you have just acquired upon it; it is
that you must do, focus the light upon it, turn it in such a
way that the thing cannot resist it.

You won't be able to succeed the very first day but you
just do it persistently and little by little or perhaps suddenly
one day it will vanish. Then you will find out after a time that
you are another person.[130]   — THE MOTHER

*

What the Mother spoke of was not self-analysis nor dissec-
tion; they are mental things which can deal with the inanimate or make the live dead — they are not spiritual methods.
What the Mother spoke of was not analysis, but a seeing of
oneself and of all the living movements of the being and the
nature, a vivid observation of the personalities and forces
that move on the stage of our being, their motives, their impulses, their potentialities, an observation quite as interesting as the seeing and understanding of a drama or a novel, a
living vision and perception of how things are done in us,
which brings also a living mastery over this inner universe.
Such things become dry only when one deals with them with
the analytic and ratiocinative mind, not when one deals with
them thus seeingly and intuitively as a movement of life. If
you had that observation (from the inner spiritual, not the
outer intellectual and ethical viewpoint), then it would be

comparatively easy for you to get out of your difficulties; for instance, you would find at once where this irrational impulse to flee away came from and it would not have any hold upon you. Of course, all that can be done to the best effect when you stand back from the play of your nature and become the Witness-Control or the Spectator-Actor-Manager. But that is what happens when you take this kind of self-seeing posture.[131]   — SRI AUROBINDO

*

To become conscious of the various movements in oneself and be aware of what one does and why one does it, is the indispensable starting-point. The child must be taught to observe, to note his reactions and impulses and their causes, to become a discerning witness of his desires, his movements of violence and passion, his instincts of possession and appropriation and domination and the background of vanity which supports them, together with their counterparts of weakness, discouragement, depression and despair.[132]

THE MOTHER

*

... there are many things in the ordinary man of which he is not conscious, because the vital hides them from the mind and gratifies them without the mind realising what is the force that is moving the action — thus things that are done under the plea of altruism, philanthropy, service, etc. are largely moved by ego which hides itself behind these justifications;

in yoga the secret motive has to be pulled out from behind the veil, exposed and got rid of. Secondly, some things are suppressed in the ordinary life and remain lying in the nature, suppressed but not eliminated; they may rise up any day or they may express themselves in various nervous forms or other disorders of the mind or vital or body without it being evident what is their real cause. This has been recently discovered by European psychologists and much emphasised, even exaggerated in a new science called psycho-analysis. Here again, in sadhana one has to become conscious of these suppressed impulses and eliminate them....[133]

SRI AUROBINDO

*

... to become conscious of anything whatever, you must will it. And when I say "will it", I don't mean saying one day, "Oh! I would like it very much", then two days later completely forgetting it.

To will it is a constant, sustained, concentrated aspiration, an almost exclusive occupation of the consciousness. This is the first step. There are many others: a very attentive observation, a very persistent analysis, a very keen discernment of what is pure in the movement and what is not.[134]

THE MOTHER

*

When one lives in the true consciousness one feels the desires outside oneself, entering from outside, from the universal lower Prakriti, into the mind and the vital parts. In the ordinary human condition this is not felt; men become aware of the desire only when it is there, when it has come inside and found a lodging or a habitual harbourage and so they think it is their own and a part of themselves. The first condition for getting rid of desire is, therefore, to become conscious with the true consciousness; for then it becomes much easier to dismiss it than when one has to struggle with it as if it were a constituent part of oneself to be thrown out from the being. It is easier to cast off an accretion than to excise what is felt as a parcel of our substance.[135]

SRI AUROBINDO

*

What is one to do to prepare oneself for the Yoga?

I replied to the person who put to me this question: "Become conscious first of all." So the person tried to become conscious and a few months later came and told me, "Oh, what a nasty present you gave me! Formerly, in my relations with people, they all used to seem so nice, I had goodwill, they were so nice towards me, and now, since becoming conscious, I see all kinds of things in myself that are not quite pretty, and at the same time I see in others things that are not at all beautiful!" I answered her, "Quite possible! If you do not want trouble, it is better not to come out of your ignorance."

The first step therefore is to find out whether one wants to see and know the truth or wants to remain comfortably in one's ignorance.[136]   — THE MOTHER

*

This reminds me of the lady who, having gradually become conscious, told me: "Before I heard you, I had trust in men, everybody was very kind, I was happy. Now that I have begun to see clearly and become conscious, I have lost all my serenity! It is awful to become conscious!"

What is to be done? — Become still more conscious.[137]

THE MOTHER

*

Sweet Mother, when can one say that one is conscious?

That is always a relative question. One is never altogether unconscious and one is never completely conscious. It is a progressive state.

But a time comes when instead of doing things automatically, impelled by a consciousness and force of which one is quite unaware — a time comes when one can observe what goes on in oneself, study one's movements, find their causes, and at the same time begin to exercise a control first over what goes on within us, then on the influence cast on us from outside which makes us act, in the beginning altogether unconsciously and almost involuntarily, but gradually more and more consciously; and the will can wake up and react. Then at that moment, the moment there is a conscious will capable of reacting, one may say, "I have become conscious." This does not mean that it is a total and perfect consciousness, it means that it is a beginning: for example, when one is able to observe all the reactions in one's being and to have a certain control over them, to let those one approves of have play, and to control, stop, annul those one doesn't approve of.

Besides, you must become aware within of something like a goal or a purpose or an ideal you want to realise; something other than the mere instinct which impels you to live without your knowing why or how. At that time you may say you are conscious, but it doesn't mean you are perfectly conscious. And moreover, this perfection is so progressive that I believe nobody can say he is perfectly conscious; he is on the way to becoming perfectly conscious, but he isn't yet.[138]

THE MOTHER

5

ORGANISATION, HARMONISATION, UNIFICATION

A human being is made of many different parts and it takes time and conscious effort to harmonise and unify all these parts.[139]   — THE MOTHER

*

Organise your life, your work, your consciousness.

Organisation consists in putting each thing in its true place.[140]

THE MOTHER

*

The centre of the human being is the psychic which is the dwelling-place of the immanent Divine. Unification means organisation and harmonisation of all the parts of the being (mental, vital and physical) around this centre, so that all the activities of the being may be the correct expression of the will of the Divine Presence.[141]   — THE MOTHER

*

... a truly harmonious personality implies a conscious arrangement of the inner individualities. This arrangement may be effected spontaneously before birth, but that is rare. The arrangement is achieved later, by means of a discipline, a proper education. But to succeed in this one must consciously take the psychic being as the centre and arrange, harmonise the various individualities around it. True harmony, inner organisation is the result of such a persistent effort.[142]   — THE MOTHER

*

Sweet Mother, how can one unify one's being?

The first step is to find, deep within oneself, behind the desires and impulses, a luminous consciousness which is always present and manifests the physical being.

Ordinarily, one becomes aware of the presence of this consciousness only when one has to face some danger or an unexpected event or a great sorrow.

One has, then, to come into conscious contact with that and learn to do so at will. The rest will follow.[143]

THE MOTHER

*

You must become aware of the points where this harmony does not exist; you must feel them and understand the contradiction between the inner consciousness and certain outer movements. You must become conscious of this first, and once you are conscious of it, you try to adapt the outer action, outer movements to the inner ideal. But first of all you must become aware of the disharmony. For there are many people who think that everything is going well; and if they are told, "No, your outer nature is in contradiction with your inner aspiration", they protest. They are not aware. Therefore, the first step is to become aware, to become conscious of what is not in tune.

To begin with, most people will say, "What is this inner consciousness you are telling me about? I don't know it!" So, obviously, they cannot establish any harmony if they are not even conscious of something within which is higher than their ordinary consciousness. This means that many preparatory stages are needed, preparatory states of awareness, before being ready for this harmonisation.

You must first of all know what the inner aim of the being is, the aspiration, the descending force, what receives it — everything must become conscious. And then, afterwards, you must look at the outer movements in the light of this inner consciousness and see what is in tune and what is not. And then, when you have seen what does not harmonise, you must gather the will and aspiration to change it and begin with the easiest part. You should not begin with the most difficult thing, you should begin with the easiest, the one you understand best, most easily, the disharmony which seems most evident to you. Then from there, gradually, you will go to the more difficult and more central things...[144]

THE MOTHER

*

We are made up of many different parts which have to be unified around the psychic being, if we are conscious of it or at least around the central aspiration. If this unification is not done, we carry this division within us.

To do this, each thought, each feeling, each sensation, each impulse, each reaction, as it manifests, must be presented in the consciousness to the central being or its aspiration. What is in accord is accepted; what is not in accord is refused, rejected or transformed.

It is a long endeavour which may take many years — but once it is done, the unification is achieved and the path becomes easy and swift.[145]   — THE MOTHER

*

... this aggregate is, because of its composition, a heterogeneous compound, not a single harmonious and homogeneous whole. This is the reason why there is a constant confusion and even a conflict in our members which our mental reason and will are moved to control and harmonise and have often much difficulty in creating out of their confusion or conflict some kind of order and guidance; even so, ordinarily, we drift too much or are driven by the stream of our nature and act from whatever in it comes uppermost at the time and seizes the instruments of thought and action, — even our seemingly deliberate choice is more of an automatism than we imagine; our co-ordination of our multifarious elements and of our consequent thoughts, feelings, impulses, actions by the reason and will is incomplete and a half-measure. In animal being Nature acts by her own mental and vital intuitions; she works out an order by the compulsion of habit and instinct which the animal implicitly obeys, so that the shiftings of its consciousness do not matter. But man cannot altogether act in the same way without forfeiting his prerogative of manhood; he cannot leave his being to be a chaos of instincts and impulses regulated by the automatism of Nature: mind has become conscious in him and is therefore self-compelled to make some attempt, however elementary in many, to see and control and in the end more and more perfectly harmonise the manifold components, the different and conflicting tendencies that seem to make up his surface being. He does succeed in setting up a sort of regulated chaos or ordered confusion in him, or at least succeeds in thinking that he is directing himself by his mind and will, even though in fact that direction is only partial; for not only a disparate consortium of habitual motive-forces but also newly emergent vital and physical tendencies and impulses, not always calculable or controllable, and many incoherent and inharmonious mental elements use his reason and will, enter into and determine his self-building, his nature-development, his life action. Man is in his self a unique Person, but he is also in his manifestation of self a multiperson; he will never succeed in being master of himself until the Person imposes itself on his multipersonality and governs it: but this can only be imperfectly done by the surface mental will and reason; it can be perfectly done only if he goes within and finds whatever central being is by its predominant influence at the head of all his expression and action. In inmost truth it is his soul that is this central being, but in outer fact it is often one or other of the part beings in him that rules, and this representative of the soul, this deputy self he can mistake for the inmost soul-principle.[146]

SRI AUROBINDO

*

This unification is indispensable if one wants to be the master of one's being and of all its actions.

It is a long and meticulous work that requires much perseverance, but the result is worth the trouble, for it brings not only mastery but also the possibility of the transformation and illumination of the consciousness.[147]   — THE MOTHER

*

What is the way to establish unity and homogeneity in our being?

Keep the will firm. Treat the recalcitrant parts as disobedient children. Act upon them constantly and patiently. Convince them of their error.

In the depths of your consciousness is the psychic being, the temple of the Divine within you. This is the centre round which should come about the unification of all these divergent parts, all these contradictory movements of your being. Once you have got the consciousness of the psychic being and its aspiration, these doubts and difficulties can be destroyed. It takes more or less time, but you will surely succeed in the end. Once you have turned to the Divine, saying, "I want to be yours", and the Divine has said, "Yes", the whole world cannot keep you from it. When the central being has made its surrender, the chief difficulty has disappeared. The outer being is like a crust. In ordinary people the crust is so hard and thick that they are not conscious of the Divine within them. If once, even for a moment only, the inner being has said, "I am here and I am yours", then it is as though a bridge has been built and little by little the crust becomes thinner and thinner until the two parts are wholly joined and the inner and the outer become one.[148]

THE MOTHER

*

You can be a different person at different moments in your life. I know people who took decisions, had a strong will, knew what they wanted and prepared to do it. Then there was a little reversal in the being; another part came up and spoilt all the work in ten minutes. What had been accomplished in two months was all undone. When the first part comes back it is in dismay, it says: "What!... " Then the whole work has to be started again, slowly. Hence it is evident that it is very important to become aware of the psychic being; one must have a kind of signpost or a mirror in which all things are reflected and show themselves as they truly are. And then, according to what they are, one puts them in one place or another; one begins to explain, to organise. That takes time. The same part comes back three or four times and every part that comes up says: "Put me in the first place; what the others do is not important, not at all important, it is I who will decide, for I am the most important." I am sure that if you look at yourself, you will see that there's not one among you who has not had the experience. You want to become conscious, to have goodwill, you have understood, your aspiration is shining — all is brilliant, illuminated; but all of a sudden something happens, a useless conversation, some unfortunate reading, and that upsets everything. Then one thinks that it was an illusion one lived in, that all things were seen from a certain angle.

This is life. One stumbles and falls at the first occasion. One tells oneself: "Oh! One can't always be so serious", and when the other part returns, once again, one repents bitterly: "I was a fool, I have wasted my time, now I must begin again.... " At times there is one part that's ill-humoured, in revolt, full of worries, and another which is progressive, full of surrender. All that, one after the other.

There is but one remedy: that signpost must always be there, a mirror well placed in one's feelings, impulses, all one's sensations. One sees them in this mirror. There are some which are not very beautiful or pleasant to look at; there are others which are beautiful, pleasant, and must be kept. This one does a hundred times a day if necessary. And it is very interesting. One draws a kind of big circle around the psychic mirror and arranges all the elements around it. If there is something that is not all right, it casts a sort of grey shadow upon the mirror: this element must be shifted, organised. It must be spoken to, made to understand, one must come out of that darkness. If you do that, you never get bored. When people are not kind, when one has a cold in the head, when one doesn't know one's lessons, and so on, one begins to look into this mirror. It is very interesting, one sees the canker. "I thought I was sincere!" — not at all.

Not a thing happens in life which is not interesting. This mirror is very, very well made. Do that for two years, three, four years, at times one must do it for twenty years. Then at the end of a few years, look back, turn your gaze upon what you were three years ago: "How I have changed!... Was I like that?... " It is very entertaining.[149]   — THE MOTHER

*

There are people who in a certain state of being are constructive, for example, and capable of organising their life and doing very useful work, and in another part of their being they are absolutely destructive and constantly demolish what the other has constructed. I knew quite a number of people of this kind who, apparently had a rather incoherent life, but it was because the two parts of the being, instead of completing each other and harmonising in a synthesis, were separated and in opposition, and one undid what the other did, and all the time they passed like this from one to the other. They had a disorganised life. And there are more people of this kind than one would think!

There are very outstanding examples, striking ones, so clear and distinct they are; but less totally opposed conditions, though all the same in opposition to one another, occur very, very often. Besides, one has oneself the experience, when one has tried to make progress; there is one part of the being which participates in the effort and makes progress, and suddenly, without rhyme or reason, all the effort one has made, all the consciousness one has gained, capsizes in something which is quite different, opposed, over which one has no control.

Some people can make an effort the whole day through, succeed in building something within themselves; they go to sleep at night and the next morning all that they had done on the previous day is lost, they have lost it in a state of unconsciousness. This happens very often, these are not exceptional cases, far from it. And this is what explains, you see, why some people — when they withdraw into their higher mind for instance — can enter into very deep meditation and be liberated from the things of this world, and then when they return to their ordinary physical consciousness, are absolutely ordinary if not even vulgar, because they haven't taken care to establish any contact, and to see that what is above acts and transforms what is below.[150]   — THE MOTHER

*

I have not attempted the unification of the different personalities which may be in me, but I have tried to put them facing each other, the good opposite the bad, and I have never found in the good a sufficient dynamism to fight against the bad.

Have you never thought that your judgment of what is "good" and "bad" was a purely human judgment? And that it might not necessarily tally with the judgment of the divine Presence within you? The "bad" things you could not get rid of were probably things not in their place, things not properly balanced, and it would be a great pity if they were eliminated because, perhaps, a part of your energy and of your divine Presence would disappear at the same time. People who do not do yoga under the direction of a guide follow ordinary moral notions and at times they feel very perplexed because with all their goodwill they do not get the expected result; that happens because generally they wish to approve of their being instead of transforming it and because moral notions are very bad. In the work of unification of the being, you must needs have imagination enough to be able to put the movements you have, the movements you wish to keep, to put them before what you are capable of imagining as most akin to the divine Presence; naturally, at first it is only an imagination quite far from the truth, but it would help you to get out a little from moral narrowness and also from the limitations of your consciousness. For example, you have the idea of putting what you are and what you do before a consciousness which is at once infinite and eternal. These two words do not perhaps make much sense at the beginning, but they compel you to break the limits and to put yourself in front of something which surpasses you so much on every side that its judgment cannot be the same as that of a human mentality. One must begin absolutely like that. If you try to analyse yourself according to moral principles, you may be sure of going contrary to the divine plan. Not that the Divine is amoral, mark that, but this is not a kind of morality that mankind understands at all, it is not the same.[151]   — THE MOTHER

*

It seems to me impossible to escape from this necessity [organisation of the being around the psychic] if one wants to be and is to be a conscious instrument of the divine Force. You may be moved, pushed into action and used as *uncon-*

scious instruments by the divine Force, if you have a minimum of goodwill and sincerity. But to become a conscious instrument, capable of identification and conscious, willed movements, you must have this inner organisation; otherwise you will always be running into a chaos somewhere, a confusion somewhere or an obscurity, an unconsciousness somewhere. And naturally your action, even though guided exclusively by the Divine, will not have the perfection of expression it has when one has acquired a conscious organisation around this divine Centre.

It is an assiduous task, which may be done at any time and under any circumstances, for you carry within yourself all the elements of the problem. You don't need anything from outside, no outer aid to do this work. But it requires great perseverance, a sort of tenacity, for very often it happens that there are bad "creases" in the being, habits — which come from all sorts of causes, which may come from atavistic malformation or also from education or from the environment you have lived in or from many other causes. And these bad creases you try to smooth out, but they wrinkle up again. And then you must begin the work over again, often, many, many, many a time, without getting discouraged, before the final result is obtained. But nothing and nobody can prevent you from doing it, nor any circumstance. For you carry within yourself the problem and the solution.

(Silence)

And to tell the truth, the most common malady humanity suffers from is boredom. Most of the stupidities men commit come from an attempt to escape boredom. Well, I say for certain that no outer means are any good, and that boredom pursues you and will pursue you no matter what you try to escape from it; but that this way, that is, beginning this work of organising your being and all its movements and all its elements around the central Consciousness and Presence, this is the surest and most complete cure, and the most comforting, for all possible boredom. It gives life a tremendous interest. And an extraordinary diversity. You no longer have the time to get bored.

Only, one must persevere.

And what adds to the interest of the thing is that this kind of work, this harmonisation and organisation of the being around the divine Centre can only be done in a physical body and on earth. That is truly the essential and original reason for physical life. For, as soon as you are no longer in a physical body, you can no longer do it *at all*.

And what is still more remarkable is that only human beings can do it, for only human beings have at their centre the divine Presence in the psychic being. For example, this work of self-development and organisation and becoming aware of all the elements is not within the reach of the beings of the vital and mental planes, nor even of the beings who are usually called "gods"; and when they want to do it, when they really want to organise themselves and become completely conscious, they have to take a body.

And yet, human beings come into a physical body without knowing why, most of them go through life without knowing why, they leave their body without knowing why, and they have to begin the same thing all over again, indefinitely, until one day, someone comes along and tells them, "Be careful! you know, there is a purpose to this. You are here for this work, don't miss your opportunity!"

And how many years are wasted.[152]   — THE MOTHER

*

... you have many sides to your personality or rather many personalities in you; it is indeed their discordant movements each getting in the way of the other, as happens when they are expressed through the external mind, that have stood much in the way of your sadhana. There is the vital personality which was turned towards success and enjoyment and got it and wanted to go on with it but could not get the rest of the being to follow. There is the vital personality that wanted enjoyment of a deeper kind and suggested to the other that it could very well give up these unsatisfactoy things if it got an equivalent in some faeryland of a higher joy. There is the psycho-vital personality that is the Vaishnava within you and wanted the Divine Krishna and bhakti and Ananda. There is the personality which is the poet and musician and a seeker of beauty through these things. There is the mental-vital personality which, when it saw the vital standing in the way, insisted on a grim struggle of Tapasya, and it is no doubt that also which approves Vairagya and Nirvana. There is the physical-mental personality which is the Russellite, extrovert, doubter. There is another mental-emotional personality all whose ideas are for belief in the Divine, yoga, bhakti, Guruvada. There is the psychic being also which has pushed you into the sadhana and is waiting for its hour of emergence.

What are you going to do with all these people? If you want Nirvana, you have either to expel them or stifle them or beat them into coma. All authorities assure us that the exclusive Nirvana business is a most difficult job (*duḥkham dehavadbhiḥ*, says the Gita), and your own attempt at suppressing the others was not encouraging, — according to your own account it left you as dry and desperate as a sucked orange, no juice left anywhere. If the desert is your way to the promised land, that does not matter. But — well, if it is not, then there is another way — it is what we call the integration, the harmonisation of the being. That cannot be done from outside, it cannot be done by the mind and vital being — they are sure to bungle their affair. It can be done only from within by the soul, the Spirit which is the centraliser, itself the centre of these radii. In all of them there is a truth that can harmonise with the true truth of the others. For there is a truth in Nirvana — Nirvana is nothing but the peace and freedom of the Spirit which can exist in itself, be there world or no world, world-order or world-disorder. Bhakti and the heart's call for the Divine have a truth — it is the truth of the divine Love and Ananda. The will for Tapasya has in it a truth — it is the truth of the Spirit's mastery over its members. The musician and poet stand for a truth, it is the truth of the expression of the Spirit through beauty. There is a truth behind the mental affirmer; even there is a truth behind the mental doubter, the Russellian, though far behind him — the truth of the denial of false forms. Even behind the two vital personalities there is a truth, the truth of the possession of the inner and outer worlds not by the ego but by the Divine.

That is the harmonisation for which our yoga stands — but it cannot be achieved by any outward arrangement, it can only be achieved by going inside and looking, willing and acting from the psychic and from the spiritual centre. For the truth of the being is there and the secret of Harmony also is there.[153]

SRI AUROBINDO

*

When humanity was first created, the ego was the unifying element. It was around the ego that the different states of being were grouped; but now that the birth of superhumanity is being prepared, the ego has to disappear and give way to the psychic being, which has slowly been formed by divine intervention in order to manifest the Divine in the human being.

It is under the psychic influence that the Divine manifests in man and thus prepares the coming of superhumanity.

The psychic is immortal and it is through the psychic that immortality can be manifested on earth.

So the important thing now is to find one's psychic, unite with it and allow it to replace the ego, which will be compelled either to get converted or disappear.[154]

THE MOTHER

6

SOME ANSWERS AND EXPLANATIONS

*(All passages in this Section have been drawn
from the works of the Mother)*

Complexity of the Being and Its Destinies

To foresee destiny! How many have attempted it, how many
systems have been elaborated, how many sciences of divi-
nation have been created and developed only to perish under the charge of charlatanism or superstition. And why is
destiny always so unforeseeable? Since it has been proved
that everything is ineluctably determined, how is it that one
cannot succeed in knowing this determinism with any certainty?

Here again the solution is to be found in Yoga. And by
yogic discipline one can not only foresee destiny but modify
it and change it almost totally. First of all, Yoga teaches us
that we are not a single being, a simple entity which necessarily has a single destiny that is simple and logical. Rather
we have to acknowledge that the destiny of most men is complex, often to the point of incoherence. Is it not this very
complexity which gives us the impression of unexpected-
ness, of indeterminacy and consequently of unpredictability?

To solve the problem one must know that, to begin with,
all living creatures, and more especially human beings, are
made up of a combination of several entities that come together, interpenetrate, sometimes organising themselves and

completing each other, sometimes opposing and contradicting one another. Each one of these beings or states of being belongs to a world of its own and carries within it its own destiny, its own determinism. And it is the combination of all these determinisms, which is sometimes very heterogeneous, that results in the destiny of the individual. But as the organisation and relationship of all these entities can be altered by personal discipline and effort of will, as these various determinisms act on each other in different ways according to the concentration of the consciousness, their combination is nearly always variable and therefore unforeseeable.

For example, the physical or material destiny of a being comes from his paternal and maternal forebears, from the physical conditions and circumstances in which he is born; one should be able to foresee the events of his physical life, his state of health and approximately how long his body will last. But then there comes into play the formation of his vital being (the being of desires and passions, but also of impulsive energy and active will) which brings with it its own destiny. This destiny affects the physical destiny and can alter it completely and often even change it for the worse. For example, if a man born with a very good physical balance, who ought to live in very good health, is driven by his vital to all kinds of excesses, bad habits and even vices, he can in this way partly destroy his good physical destiny and lose the harmony of health and strength which would have been his but for this unfortunate interference. This is only one example. But the problem is much more complex, for, to the physical and vital destinies, there must be added the mental destiny, the psychic destiny, and many others besides.

In fact, the higher a being stands on the human scale, the more complex is his being, the more numerous are his destinies and the more unforeseeable his fate seems to be as a consequence. This is however only an appearance. The knowledge of these various states of being and their corresponding inner worlds gives at the same time the capacity to discern the various destinies, their interpenetration and their combined or dominant action. Higher destinies are quite obviously the closest to the central truth of the universe, and if they are allowed to intervene, their action is necessarily beneficent. The art of living would then consist in maintaining oneself in one's highest state of consciousness and thus allowing one's highest destiny to dominate the others in life and action. So one can say without any fear of making a mistake: be always at the summit of your consciousness and the best will always happen to you. But that is a maximum which is not easy to reach. If this ideal condition turns out to be unrealisable, the individual can at least, when he is confronted by a danger or a critical situation, call upon his highest destiny by aspiration, prayer and trustful surrender to the divine will. Then, in proportion to the sincerity of his call, this higher destiny intervenes favourably in the normal destiny of the being and changes the course of events insofar as they concern him personally. It is events of this kind that appear to the outer consciousness as miracles, as divine interventions.[155]

Body Formation and Character

Mother, does a person's body-formation express his character?

No. Even the character itself is not a simple affair, that is, the character of a person is not the expression of his true being but the result of many things. For example, atavism may be expressed, that is, what comes from the father, the mother, from both together which may have a different result; from what has gone before them — the past history, grandfathers, great-grandfathers, etc.; and then from the environment in which people have lived when they were very young and had no independence at all. That has a considerable effect on the character. And this character affects the physical formation. So, just by seeing somebody one cannot quite say what his true nature is. One may describe his tendencies, know his difficulties, his possibilities, but it is only with the growth of the consciousness and as the development becomes voluntary and organised that the body can begin to express the true character of the person.[156]

Atavistic Elements in One's Make-Up

Is the vital distorted from the very birth?

If your birth has not been accidental, you could very well think there was no distortion, but what you are at your birth is most of the time almost absolutely what your mother and father have made you, and also, through them, what your grandparents have made you. There are certain vital traditions in families and, besides, there is the state of consciousness in which you were formed, conceived — the moment at which you were conceived — and that, not once in a million times does that state conform to true aspiration; and it is only a true aspiration which could make your vital pure of all mixture, make the vital element attracted for the formation of the being a pure element, free from all contagion; I mean that if a psychic being enters there, it can gather elements favourable to its growth. In the world as it is, things are so mixed up, have been so mixed up in every way, that it is almost impossible to have elements of the vital sufficiently pure not to suffer the contagion of all other contaminated beings.

I think I have already spoken about that, I have said what kind of aspiration ought to be there in the parents before the birth; but as I said, this does not happen even once in a hundred thousand instances. The willed conception of a child is extremely rare; mostly it is an accident. Among innumerable parents it is quite a small minority that even simply bothers about what a child could be; they do not even know that what the child will be depends on what they are. It is a very small élite which knows this. Most of the time things go as they can; anything at all happens and people don't even realise what is happening. So, in these conditions how do you expect to be born with a vital being sufficiently pure to be of help to you? One is born with a slough to clean before one begins to live. And once you have made a good start on the way to the inner transformation and you go down to the subconscient root of the being — that exactly which comes from parents, from atavism — well, you do see what it is! All, almost all difficulties are there, there are very few things added to existence after the first years of life. This happens at any odd moment; if you keep bad company or read bad books, the poison may enter you; but there are all the imprints deep-rooted in the subconscient, the dirty habits you have and against which you struggle. For instance, there are people who can't open their mouth without telling a lie, and they don't always do this deliberately (that is the worst of it), or people who can't come in touch with others without quarrel-ling, all sorts of stupidities — they are there in the subcon-scient, deeply rooted. Now, when you have a goodwill, externally you do your best to avoid all that, to correct it if possible; you work, you fight; then become aware that this thing always keeps coming up, it comes up from some part which escapes your control. But if you enter this subconscient, if you let your consciousness infiltrate it, and look carefully, gradually you will discover all the sources, all the origins of all your difficulties; then you will begin to understand what your fathers and mothers, grandfathers and grandmothers were, and if at a certain moment you are unable to control yourself, you will understand, "I am like that because they were like that."

If you have within you a psychic being sufficiently awake to watch over you, to prepare your path, it can draw towards you things which help you, draw people, books, circum-stances, all sorts of little coincidences which come to you as though brought by some benevolent will and give you an indication, a help, a support to take decisions and turn you in the right direction. But once you have taken this decision, once you have decided to find the truth of your being, once you start sincerely on the road, then everything seems to conspire to help you to advance, and if you observe carefully you see gradually the source of your difficulties: "Ah! Wait a minute, this failing was in my father; oh! this habit was my mother's; oh! my grandmother was like this, my grandfather was like that" or it could well be the nurse who took care of you when you were small, or brothers and sisters who played with you, the little friends you met, and you will find that all this was there, in this person or that or the other. But if you continue to be sincere, you find you can cross all this quite calmly, and after a time you cut all the moorings with which you were born, break the chains and go freely on the path.

If you really want to transform your character, it is that you must do. It has always been said that it is impossible to change one's nature; in all books of philosophy, even of yoga, you are told the same story: "You cannot change your character, you are born like that, you are like that." This is absolutely false, I guarantee it is false; but there is something very difficult to do to change your character, because it is not your character which must be changed, it is the character of your antecedents. In them you will not change it (because they have no such intention), but it is in you that it must be changed. It is what they have given you, all the little gifts made to you at your birth — nice gifts — it is this which must be changed. But if you succeed in getting hold of the thread of these things, the true thread, since you have worked upon this with perseverance and sincerity, one fine morning you will be free; all this will fall off from you and you will be able to get a start in life without any burden. Then you will be a new man, living a new life, almost with a new nature. And if you look back you will say, "It is not possible, I was never like that!"[157]

Individuality Is a Conquest

"The limitations of the body are a mould; soul and mind have to pour themselves into them, break them and constantly remould them in wider limits till the formula of agreement is found between this finite and their own infinity."   — Sri Aurobindo, *Thoughts and Glimpses*

Sweet Mother, how should we understand: "the limitations of the body are a mould"?

If you did not have a body with a precise form, if you were not a formed individuality, fully conscious and having its own qualities, you would all be fused into one another and be indistinguishable. Even if we go only a little inwards, into the most material vital being, there is such a mixture between the vibrations of different people that it is very difficult to distinguish any of you. And if you did not have a body, it would be a sort of inextricable pulp. Therefore, it is the form, this precise and apparently rigid form of the body, which distinguishes you one from another. So this form serves as a mould. (*Speaking to the child*) Do you know what a mould is? — Yes! One pours something inside, in a liquid or semi-liquid form, and when it cools down one can break the mould and have the object in a precise form. Well, the form of the body serves as a mould in which the vital and mental forces can take a precise form, so that you can become an individual being separate from others.

It is only gradually, very slowly, through the movements of life and a more or less careful and thorough education that you begin to have sensations which are personal to you, feelings and ideas which are personal to you. An individualised mind is something extremely rare, which comes only after a long education; otherwise it is a kind of thought-current passing through your brain and then through another's and then through a multitude of other brains, and all this is in perpetual movement and has no individuality. One thinks what others are thinking, others think what still others are thinking, and everybody thinks like that in a great mixture, because these are currents, vibrations of thought passing from one to another. If you look at yourself attentively, you will very quickly become aware that very few thoughts in you are personal. Where do you draw them from? — From what you have heard, from what you have read, what you have been taught, and how many of these thoughts you have are the result of your own experience, your own reflection, your purely personal observation? — Not many.

Only those who have an intense intellectual life, who are in the habit of reflecting, observing, putting ideas together, gradually form a mental individuality for themselves.

Most people — and not only those who are uneducated but even the well-read — can have the most contradictory, the most opposite ideas in their heads without even being aware of the contradictions. I have seen numerous examples like that, of people who cherished ideas and even had political, social, religious opinions on all the so-called higher fields of human intelligence, who had absolutely contradictory opinions on the same subject, and were not aware of it. And if you observe yourself, you will see that you have many ideas which ought to be linked by a sequence of intermediate ideas which are the result of a considerable widening of the thought if they are not to coexist in an absurd way.

Therefore, before an individuality becomes truly individual and has its own qualities, it must be contained in a vessel, otherwise it would spread out like water and would no longer have any form at all. Some people, at a rather lower level, know themselves only by the name they bear. They would not be able to distinguish themselves from their neighbours except by their name. They are asked, "Who are you?" — "My name is this." A little later they tell you the name of their occupation or about their main characteristic. If they are asked, "Who are you?" — "I am a painter."

But at a certain level the only answer is the name....

One lives by a kind of habit which is barely half-conscious — one lives, does not even objectify what one does, why one does it, how one does it. One does it by habit. All those who are born in a certain environment, a certain country, automatically take the habits of that environment, not only material habits but habits of thought, habits of feeling and habits of acting. They do it without watching themselves doing it, quite naturally, and if someone points this out to them they are astonished.

As a matter of fact, one has the habit of sleeping, speaking, eating, moving and one does all this as something quite natural, without wondering why or how.... And many other things. All the time one does things automatically, by force of habit, one does not watch oneself. And so, when one lives in a particular society, one automatically does what is normally done in that society. And if somebody begins to watch himself acting, watch himself feeling and thinking, he looks like a kind of phenomenal monster compared with the environment he lives in.

Therefore, individuality is not at all the rule, it is an exception, and if you do not have that sort of bag, a particular form which is your outer body and your appearance, you could hardly be distinguished from one another.

Individuality is a conquest. And, as Sri Aurobindo says here, this first conquest is only a first stage, and once you have realised within you something like a personal independent and conscious being, then what you have to do is to break the form and go farther. For example, if you want to progress mentally, you must break all your mental forms, all your mental constructions to be able to make new ones. So, to begin with, a tremendous labour is required to individualise oneself, and afterwards one must demolish all that has been done in order to progress. But as you do not watch yourself doing things and as it is the custom — not everywhere, of course; let us say here — the custom to work, to read, to develop yourself, to try to do something, to form yourself a little, you do it quite naturally and without even watching yourself, as I said.

And only when these external forms come into a mutual friction you begin to feel that you are different from others. Otherwise you are this person or that, according to the name you bear. It is only when there is a friction, when something does not go smoothly, that you become aware of a difference, then you see that you are different, otherwise you are not aware of it and you are not different. In fact, you are very, very little different from one another.

How many things in your life are done at least essentially in the same way as others. For instance, sleeping, moving and eating, and all sorts of things like that. Never have you asked yourselves why you do a thing in one way and not another. You wouldn't be able to say. If I asked you, "Why do you act in this way and not that?" you wouldn't know what to say. But it is quite simply because you were born in certain conditions and it is the habit to be like that in these conditions. Otherwise, if you had been born in another age and other conditions, you would act altogether differently without even realising the difference, it would appear absolutely natural to you.... For instance — a very, very small instance — in most Western countries and even in some Eastern ones, people sew like this, from right to left; in Japan they sew from left to right. Well, it seems quite natural to you to sew from right to left, doesn't it? That is how you have been taught and you don't think about it, you sew in that way. If you go to Japan and they see you sewing, it makes them laugh, for they are in the habit of sewing differently. It is the same thing with writing. You write like this, from left to right, but there are people who write from top to bottom, and others who write from right to left, and they do it most naturally. I am not speaking of those who have studied, reflected, compared ways of writing, I am not speaking of more or less learned people, no, I am speaking of quite ordinary people, and above all of children who do what is done around them, quite spontaneously and without questioning. But then, when by chance or circumstance they are faced with a different way, it is a tremendous revelation for them that things can be done in a different way from theirs.

And these are quite simple things, I mean the ones which strike you, but this is true down to the smallest detail. You do things in this way because in the place and environment in which you live they are done in this way. And you do not watch yourself doing them.

Indeed, the source was One, you see, and creation had to be manifold. And it must have represented quite a considerable labour to make this multiplicity conscious of being multiple.

And if one observes very attentively, if creation had kept the memory of its origin, it would perhaps never have become a diverse multiplicity. There would have been at the centre of each being the sense of perfect unity, and the diversity would — perhaps — never have been expressed.

Through the loss of the memory of this unity began the possibility of becoming conscious of differences; and when one goes into the inconscient, at the other end, one falls back into a sort of unity that's unconscious of itself, in which the diversity is as unexpressed as it is in the origin.

At both ends there is the same absence of diversity. In one case it is through a supreme consciousness of unity, in the other through a perfect unconsciousness of unity.

The fixity of form is the means by which individuality can be formed.[158]

The Ordinary State of People —
Identification and Dispersion

One is always identified more or less with all that one does and all the things with which one is in contact. The ordinary state of people is to be in everything that they do, all that they see, all whom they frequently meet. They are like that. There is something in them which in fact is very vague and very inconsistent, and which moves around everywhere. And if they simply want to know a little what they are, they are obliged to pull back towards them a heap of things which are scattered everywhere. There is a kind of unconscious fluidity between people, I have told you this I don't know how many times; it produces a mixture, all that, as soon as it is no longer altogether material.... It's because you have a skin that you don't enter into one another like that; other-wise even the subtle physical, you see... like a kind of al-most perceptible vapour which goes out from bodies, which is the subtle physical, it intermingles terribly, and it pro-duces all kinds of reactions, constantly, of one person upon another.

One may without knowing why, without having the least idea of the cause, pass precisely from a harmony of good health to a disequilibrium and a great uneasiness! One doesn't know why, there is no outer cause, suddenly it happens; one may have been peaceful, content, in at least a pleasant, tolerable condition, then all of a sudden to become furious, discon-tented, uneasy! One doesn't know why, there is no reason. One may have been full of joy, gaiety, enthusiasm, and then, without any apparent reason, one is sad, morose, depressed, discouraged! It happens sometimes that one is in a state of depression, and then one passes on somewhere and everything is lit up: a light, a joy, why! one becomes suddenly optimistic; this of course is rare — it can also happen, it is the same thing, it is also contagious; but still one risks much more catching destructive rather than constructive things.

There are very few people who carry with them an atmosphere which irradiates joy, peace, confidence; it is very rare. But these are truly benefactors of humanity. They don't need to open their mouth.[159]

Why Man Questions Himself

"Because the tiger acts according to his nature and knows not anything else, therefore he is divine and there is no evil in him. If he questioned himself, then he would be a criminal."
— Sri Aurobindo

What would be the truly natural state for man? Why does he question himself?

On earth* man is a transitional being. Therefore, in the course of his evolution, he has had several natures in succession, which have followed an ascending curve and will continue to follow it until he reaches the threshold of the

---

* Mother added: "This precise detail is not superfluous; I said 'on earth' meaning that man does not belong merely to earth: in essence man is a universal being, but he has a special manifestation on earth."

supramental nature and is transformed into the superman. This curve is the spiral of mental development.

We tend to call "natural" any spontaneous manifestation which is not the result of a choice or a preconceived decision, that is to say, without the intrusion of any mental activity. This is why when a man has a vital spontaneity which is very little mentalised, he seems more "natural" in his simplicity. But this naturalness is very much like that of the animal and is at the very bottom of the human evolutionary scale. He will only regain this spontaneity free from mental intrusion when he attains to the supramental stage, that is to say, when he transcends mind and emerges into the higher Truth.

Until then all his behaviour is, naturally, natural! But with the mind evolution has become, one cannot say twisted, but distorted, because by its very nature the mind was open to perversion and almost from the beginning it became perverted, or, to be more precise, it was perverted by the Asuric forces. And this state of perversion gives us the impression that it is unnatural.

Why does he question himself? Simply because this is the nature of the mind!

With the mind individualisation began and a very acute feeling of separation, and also a kind of impression, more or less precise, of freedom of choice — all that, all these psychological states are the natural consequences of mental life and they open the door to everything we see now, from aberrations to the most rigorous principles. Mind has the impression that it can choose between one thing and another, but this impression is the distortion of a true principle which would be completely realisable only when the soul or psychic being appears in the consciousness and if the soul were to take up the governance of the being. Then man's life would truly become the manifestation of the supreme Will expressing itself individually, consciously. But in the normal human state this is something extremely exceptional which to the ordinary human consciousness does not seem at all natural — it seems almost supernatural!

Man questions himself because the mental instrument is intended to see all possibilities. And the immediate consequence of this is the concept of good and evil, or of what is right and what is wrong, and all the miseries that follow from that. One cannot say that it is a bad thing; it is an intermediate stage — not a very pleasant one, but still... one which was certainly inevitable for the complete development of the mind.[160]

What One Calls "Myself"

Sweet Mother, when you say, "Concentrate in the heart", does it mean concentrate with the mind?

The consciousness, not the mind, the consciousness!

I don't say think in the heart, I say concentrate, concentrate the energy, concentrate the consciousness, concentrate the aspiration, concentrate the will. *Concentrate.* One can have an extremely intense concentration without a single thought, and in fact it is usually much more intense when one doesn't think. (*Silence*) It's one of the most indispensable things to do if one wants to succeed in having self-control and even a limited self-knowledge: to be able to localise one's consciousness and move it about in the different parts of one's being, in such a way as to distinguish between one's consciousness and one's thought, feelings, impulses, become aware of what the consciousness is in itself. And in this way one can learn how to shift it: one can put one's consciousness in the body, put it in the vital, put it in the psychic (that's the best place to put it in); one can put one's consciousness in the mind, can raise it above the mind, and with one's consciousness one can go into all the regions of the universe.

But first of all one must know what one's consciousness is, that is, become conscious of one's consciousness, localise it. And for this there are many exercises. But one of them is very well known, it is to observe oneself and watch oneself living, and then see whether it is really the body which is the consciousness of the being, what one calls "myself"; and then when one has realised that it is not at all the body, that the body expresses something else, then one searches in his impulses, emotions, to see whether it's that, and again one finds out that it is not that; and then one seeks in his thoughts, whether the thought is truly himself, what he calls "myself", and at the end of a very short time one becomes aware: "No, I am thinking, therefore 'myself' is different from my thoughts." And so, by progressive eliminations one succeeds in entering into contact with something, something which gives you the impression of being — "Yes, that's 'myself'. And this something I can move around, I can move it from my body to my vital, to my mind, I can even, if I am very... how to put it?... very practised in moving it, I can move it into other people, and it's in this way that I can identify my-self with things and people. I can with the help of my aspira-tion make it come out of my human form, rise above towards regions which are no longer this little body at all and what it contains." And so one begins to understand what one's con-sciousness is; and it's after that that one can say, "Good, I shall unite my consciousness with my psychic being and shall leave it there, so that it may be in harmony with the Divine and be able to surrender entirely to the Divine." Or else, "If by this exercise of rising above my faculties of thinking and my intellect I can enter a region of pure light, pure knowl-edge..." then one can put his consciousness there and live like that, in a luminous splendour which is above the physical form.

But first this consciousness must be mobile, and one must know how to distinguish it from the other parts of the being which in fact are its instruments, its modes of expression. The consciousness must make use of these things, and not you mistake these things for the consciousness. You put the con-sciousness in these things, so you become conscious of your body, conscious of your vital, conscious of your mind, con-scious of all your activities through your will for identifica-tion; but for this, first your consciousness must not be com-pletely entangled, mingled, joined, so to say, with all these things, it must not take them for itself, must not be mistaken.

When one thinks of himself (obviously out of millions of men perhaps there are not ten who do otherwise) he thinks "Myself... that's my body, that's what I call 'myself', what's like this. And so, I am like that; and then my neighbour, he also is the body. When I speak of another person, I speak of his body." And so, as long as one is in this state he is plaything of all possible movements and has no self-control.

The body is the last instrument and yet it's this which one calls "myself" most of the time, unless one has begun to reflect.[161]

The Truth of the Being

There is something I was asked some time ago to which I have not yet replied. It is this. I have written somewhere:

"The absolute of every being is its unique relation with the Divine and its unique manner of expressing the Divine in the manifestation."

This is what is called here in India the truth of the being or the law of the being, the *dharma* of the being: the centre and the cause of the individuality.

Everyone carries his truth within himself, a truth which is unique, which is altogether his own and which he must express in his life. Now what is this truth? This is the question I have been asked:

> *"What is this truth of the being, and how is it expressed*
> *externally in physical life?"*

It is expressed in this way: each individual being has a direct and unique relation with the Supreme, the Origin, That which is beyond all creation. It is this unique relation which must be expressed in one's life, through a unique mode of being in relation with the Divine. Therefore, each one is directly and exclusively in relation with the Divine — the relation one has with the Divine is unique and exclusive; so that you receive from the Divine, when you are in a receptive state, the *totality* of the relation it is *possible* for you to have, and this is neither a sharing nor a part nor a repetition, but exclusively and uniquely *the* relation which each one can have with the Divine. So, from the psychological point of view, one is *all alone* in having this direct relation with the Divine.

One is all alone with the Supreme.

The relation one has with Him will never have an equal, will never be exactly the same as another's. No two are the same and therefore *nothing* can be taken away from you to be given to another, *nothing* can be withdrawn from you to be given to another. And if this relation disappeared from the creation, it would really disappear — which is impossible.

And this means that if one lives in the truth of one's being, one is an indispensable part of the creation. Naturally, I don't mean if one lives what one *believes* one should be, I am saying if one lives the truth of one's being; if, by a development, one is able to enter into contact with the truth of one's being, one is immediately in a unique and exclusive relation with the Divine, which hasn't its equal.

There, now.

And naturally, because it is the truth of your being, that is what you should express in your life.[162]

The Shadow

You have said: "Everyone possesses... two opposite tendencies of character,... which are like the light and the shadow of the same thing."* Why are things made in this way? Can't one have only the light?

Yes, if one eliminates the shadow. But it must be eliminated. That does not happen by itself. The world as it is is a mixed world. You cannot have an object which gets the light from one side without its casting a shadow on the other. It is like that, and indeed it is the shadows which make you see the lights. The world is like that, and to have only the light one must definitely go through the entire discipline necessary for eliminating the shadow. This is what I have explained a little farther; I have said that this shadow was like a sign of what you had to conquer in your nature in order to be able to realise what you have come to do. If you have a part to play, a mission to fulfil, you will always carry in yourself

* "...Everyone possesses in a large measure, and the exceptional individual in an increasing degree of precision, two opposite tendencies of character, in almost equal proportions, which are like the light and the shadow of the same thing. Thus someone who has the capacity of being exceptionally generous will suddenly find an obstinate avarice rising up in his nature, the courageous man will be a coward in some part of his being and the good man will suddenly have wicked impulses. In this way life seems to endow everyone not only with the possibility of expressing an ideal, but also with contrary elements representing in a concrete manner the battle he has to wage and the victory he has to win for the realisation to become possible. Consequently, all life is an education pursued more or less consciously, more or less willingly." — The Mother, *Questions and Answers*, 1954 the main difficulty preventing you from realising it, so that you have within your reach the victory you must win. If you had to fight against a difficulty which is everywhere on earth, it would be very difficult (you would need to have a very vast consciousness and a very great power), while if you carry in your own nature just the shadow or defect you must conquer, well, it is there, within your reach: you see all the time the effects of this thing and can fight it directly, immediately. It is a very practical organisation.

You haven't seen in the *Bulletin* that letter of Sri Aurobindo's: the "Evil Persona"*? It is in the *Bulletin*. The thing is very well explained there.[163]

* The "Evil Persona"

What you say about the "Evil Persona" interests me greatly as it answers to my consistent experience that a person greatly endowed for the work has, always or almost always, — perhaps one ought not to make a too rigid universal rule about these things — a being attached to him, sometimes appearing like a part of him, which is just the contradiction of the thing he centrally represents in the work to be done. Or, if it is not there at first, not bound to his personality, a force of this kind enters into his environment as soon as he begins his movement to realise. Its business seems to be to oppose, to create stumblings and wrong conditions, in a word, to set before him the whole problem of the work he has started to do. It would seem as if the problem could not, in the occult economy of things, be solved otherwise than by the predestined instrument making the difficulty his own. That would explain many things that seem very disconcerting on the surface.

                                        Sri Aurobindo, *Letters on Yoga*

Becoming Aware of the Highest in Oneself

How can one become aware of the central will?

Ah, this of course is another side of the problem. First of all one must become aware of what is highest, most true, most universal and eternal in one's consciousness.

This is learnt gradually. One learns to discern among one's ordinary, external movements and the different gradations of the movements of one's inner consciousness. And if one continues to do this with a certain persistence, one realises what it is that puts this highest part of one's being into motion, which represents the ideal of the being. There is no other way. Sometimes this awakens through reading something, sometimes through a conversation, sometimes through a more or less dramatic, that is, unexpected event, which gives you a shock, shakes you up, brings you out of your usual little rut. Sometimes when you are in very great danger, suddenly you feel as though you are above yourself and beyond your small habitual weakness, having within you something higher which can hold out against circumstances.

Such occasions make you enter, first, into contact with that. Afterwards by a methodical discipline you can make the contact continuous; but usually this takes time. But first you get it like that, suddenly, for one reason or another.

(Long silence)

This may come with a very strong emotion, with a very great sorrow, a very great enthusiasm. When one is called to perform a fairly exceptional action, in circumstances which are a little exceptional, all of a sudden, one feels something as though breaking or opening within him, and one feels as though he were dominating himself, as though he had climbed up a higher rung and from there was looking at his own existence with the habitual senses. Once one has experienced this, one does not forget; even if only once it has happened, one does not forget it. And one can by concentration reproduce the state at will, later. This is the first step to cultivate it.

Afterwards one can very easily call up this state each time a decision is to be taken, and then one takes it in full awareness of the implications and foreseeing everything that's going to happen. I don't think there's one individual in the world who hasn't experienced it — in any case one cultured individual — at least once in his life, something that breaks and opens... and one understands. This seems to astonish you very much!... (*To a child*) You have never felt this, you? Yes?

I don't know.

You are not sure! (*Long silence*)

When one has had it one feels that one has begun to live, that before this one did not know what life was. Suddenly one has entered fully into life. This is not forgotten.[164]

Witnesses in the Being

What is the meaning of "the mental witness"?

The witness we have spoken about several times already, only here it is in the mind.

There are witnesses everywhere. It is a capacity of the being to detach itself, to stand back and look at what is happening, as when one looks at something happening in the street or when one looks at others playing and does not himself play, one remains seated, looking at the others moving but does not move. That's how it is.

In all the parts of the being there is one side which can do this: put itself at the back, remain quiet and look, without participating. This is what is called the witness. One has many witnesses inside oneself, and often one is a witness without even being aware of it. And if you develop this, it always gives you the possibility of being quiet and not being affected by things. One detaches oneself from them, looks at them as at a dramatic scene, without participating in it. This does not change things very much.[165]

Need for Establishing a Relation between the Outer and the Inner

"The disadvantage [of trance or *Samadhi*] is that trance becomes indispensable and the problem of the waking consciousness is not solved; it remains imperfect."

Sri Aurobindo, *Bases of Yoga*

"Waking consciousness is not solved"?

And naturally! Because if in order to have a meditation or a relation with the inner world, you are obliged to enter into *samādhi*, your waking consciousness always remains what it is, without ever changing. That's what I said in other words, you see, when I said that people have a higher consciousness only in very deep meditation. When they come out of their meditation they are no better than they were before. All their defects are there which come back as soon as they come back into their waking consciousness; and they never make any progress because they do not establish a relation between their deeper consciousness, the truth of their being, and their outer being. You see, they take off their outer being as though they were taking off a cloak, and they put it in a corner: "Come now, don't trouble me, keep quiet. You are a nuisance." And then they enter into contemplation, their meditation, into their deep experience; and then they come back, put on the cloak which of course has not changed — which perhaps is dirtier still than before — and they remain exactly as they were without any meditation.

If you want the outer being to change, it is while remaining conscious of it that you should have the other experiences; and you must not lose contact with your ordinary outer consciousness if you want it to profit by the experience. There are many people... I knew people like that, who used to meditate for hours, almost all the time... they spent their time meditating, and then if by chance... if someone disturbed them in their meditation, if they had to do something, they flew into a rage, a fury, they abused everybody, they became more intolerable than if they had never meditated, than any ordinary person. This happened because they neglected making their outer being participate in their deeper life. They cut themselves into two, so there is a portion inside which progresses and a portion outside which becomes worse and worse, because it is completely neglected.[166]

Need for Perfecting the Instruments of Consciousness

There are two things to be considered: consciousness and the instruments through which consciousness manifests. Let us take the instruments: there is the mental being which produces thoughts, the emotional being which produces feeling, the vital being which produces the power of action and the physical being that acts.

The man of genius may use anything at all and make something beautiful because he has genius; but give this genius a perfect instrument and he will make something wonderful. Take a great musician; well, even with a wretched piano and missing notes, he will produce something beautiful; but give him a good piano, well-tuned, and he will do something still more beautiful. The consciousness is the same in either case but for expression it needs a good instrument — a body with mental, vital, psychic and physical capacities.

If physically you are badly built, badly set up, it will be difficult for you, even with a good training, to do gymnastics as well as one with a beautiful well-built body. It is the same with the mind — one who has a well-organised mind, complex, complete, refined, will express himself much better than one who has a rather mediocre or badly organised mind. First of all, you must educate your consciousness, become conscious of yourself, organise your consciousness according to your ideal, but at the same time do not neglect the instruments which are in your body.

Take an example. You are in your body with your deepest ideal but you find yourself before a school class and you have to teach something to the students. Well, this light is up there, this light of consciousness, but when you have to explain to your class the science you have to teach, is it more convenient to have a fund of knowledge or will the inspiration be such that you will not need this fund of knowledge? What is your personal experience?... You find, don't you, that there are days when everything goes well — you are eloquent, your students listen to you and understand you easily. But there are other days when what you have to teach does not come, they do not listen to you — that is, you are bored and are boring. This means that in the former case your consciousness is awake and concentrated upon what you are doing, while in the second it is more or less asleep — you are left to your most external means. But in this case, if you have a fund of knowledge you can tell your students something; if you have a mind trained, prepared, a good instrument responding well when you want to make use of it, and if you have also gathered all necessary notes and notions all will go very well. But if you have nothing in your head and, besides, you are not in contact with your higher consciousness, then you have no other recourse than to take a book and read out your lesson — you will be obliged to make use of someone else's mind.

Take games. There too you find days when everything goes well; you have done nothing special previously, but even so you succeed in everything; but if you have practised well beforehand, the result is still more magnificent. If, for example, you find yourself facing someone who has trained himself slowly, seriously, with patience and endurance, and who all of a sudden has a strong aspiration, well, this one will beat you in spite of your aspiration unless your aspiration is very much superior to that of your adversary. If you have opposite you someone who knows only the technique of the game but has no conscious aspiration, whilst you are in a fully conscious state, evidently it is you who will defeat him because the quality of consciousness is superior to the quality of technique. But one cannot replace the other. The one which is superior is more important, granted but you must also also have nerves which respond quickly, spontaneous movements; you must know all the secrets of the game to be able to play perfectly. You must have both the things. What is higher is the consciousness which enables you to make the right movement at the right moment but it is not exclusive. When you seek perfection, you must not neglect the one under the pretext that you have the other.[167]

Asceticism and Self-Mastery

Mother, for self-mastery are not the ascetic methods useful sometimes?

No! You cure nothing. You only give yourself the illusion

that you have progressed, but you cure nothing. The proof is that if you stop your ascetic methods, the thing is even stronger than before; it comes back with a vengeance. It depends upon what you call ascetic methods. If it is not to indulge in satisfying all your desires, this indeed is not asceticism, it is common sense. It is something else. Ascetic methods are things like repeated fasting, compelling yourself to endure the cold... in fact, to torture your body a little. This indeed gives you only a spiritual pride, nothing more. It masters nothing at all. It is infinitely easier. People do it because it is very easy, it is simple. Just because the pride is quite satisfied and the vanity can get puffed up, it becomes very easy. One makes a great demonstration of his ascetic virtues, and so considers himself an extremely important personage, and that helps him to endure many things.

It is much more difficult to master one's impulses quietly, composedly, and to prevent them from showing themselves — much more! — without taking ascetic measures. It is much more difficult not to be attached to the things you possess than to possess nothing. This is something that has been known for centuries. It requires a much greater quality not to be attached to the things one possesses than to be without any possessions or to reduce one's possessions to a strict minimum. It is much more difficult. It is a much higher degree of moral worth. Simply this attitude: when a thing comes to you, to take it, use it; when for one reason or another it goes away, to let it go and not regret it. Not to refuse it when it comes, to know how to adapt yourself and not to regret it when it goes.[168]

Features of a "World Personality"

"What are the characteristic features of a world-personality?"

The most characteristic feature is precisely this change of consciousness. Instead of feeling like a little, isolated person, separated from others, one feels one is a universal person, containing all others and intimately united and identified with all others.

And I am asked:

"How does this person speak and act?"

Speak!... The question is not very well put, for if you ask how he speaks, well, he speaks as everybody does, with his voice, his tongue, his mouth and with words! If you were to ask what is the nature of what he says... obviously, if he expresses the state of consciousness in which he lives, he expresses a universal state of consciousness, and seeing things in a different way from ordinary men, he will express them differently, in accordance with what he sees and feels. As for acting... if all the parts of his being are in harmony, his action will obviously express his state of consciousness.

Now, there are people who have very decisive experiences in one part of their being, but these are not necessarily translated, or at least not immediately, in the other parts of their being. It is possible that through sadhana or concentration or through Grace, somebody has attained the consciousness of a world-personality, but that he still continues to act physically in quite an ordinary, nondescript way, because he has not taken care to unify his whole being, and though one part of his being is universally conscious, as soon as he begins to eat, to sleep, walk, act, he does this like all human animals. That may happen. So, it is again a purely personal question, it depends on each one, on his stage of development.

But if it is someone who has taken care to unify his being, to identify all its parts with the central truth, then naturally he will act with a total absence of egoism, with an understanding of others, an understanding which comes to him from his identification with others — and so he will act like a sage. But that depends on the care he has taken to unify his whole being around the central consciousness.

For example, to take the most positively material things like food and sleep: it is quite possible that, if he has not taken care to infuse, as it were, his new consciousness into his body, his need for food and sleep will remain almost the same and that he won't have much control over them. On the other hand, if he has taken care to unify his being and has infused his consciousness into the elements constituting his body, well, his sleep will be a conscious sleep and of a universal kind; he will be able to know at will what goes on here or anywhere, in this person or that other, in this corner of the world or any other; and his consciousness, being universal, will naturally put him in contact with all the things he wants to know. Instead of having a sleep that's unconscious and useless, except from a purely material point of view, he will have a productive and altogether conscious sleep.

For food it will be the same thing. Instead of being a slave to his needs, usually in almost entire igorance of what he needs, well, he will be perfectly conscious, at once of the needs of his body and the means of governing them. He will be able to control his needs and rule them, transform them according to the necessity of what he wants to do.[169]

Is Personal Effort Always Egoistic?
Distinction between "Selfish" and "Egoistic"

There may be an effort which is not at all selfish and is yet egoistic, because the moment it becomes personal it is egoistic — that means, it is based on the ego. But this does not mean that it is not generous, compassionate, unselfish nor that it is for narrow personal ends. It is not like that. It may be for a very unselfish work. But so long as an ego is there it is egoistic. And so long as the sense of one's own personality is there, it is naturally something egoistic; it is founded on the presence of the ego.

And this must last for a fairly long time, because it must last until the individuality is completely formed, until it has reached a certain state of individual perfection; then the presence of the ego is no longer necessary — but not before one has attained the maximum individual development.

It is not just a tiny little job. It asks for much time and much effort. And when one has attained the perfection of his own development, when one is an individual being who is truly personal, that is, who has all the characteristics of something different from all others — for in principle there are no two individualities exactly alike in the world — then, when one has succeeded in expressing the individuality one is, is exclusively, represents exclusively in the universal creation, then one is ready for the ego to disappear — but not before.

It asks for a certain length of time, not a little effort, a fairly complete education. But one may be quite unselfish long before being ready not to have the ego any longer. That is something else.[170]

Recognising Another's Soul; Looking at Oneself

Sweet Mother, with the human mind is it possible to recognise another person's soul?

Things are not so clear-cut and separate as they are in speaking; that is just why it is quite difficult to see very distinctly and clearly in oneself the different parts of the being, unless one has had a very long training and a long discipline of study and observation. There are no watertight compartments between the soul and the mind, the vital and even the physical. There is an infiltration of the soul into the mind. In some people it is even quite considerable, it is perceptible. So, the part of the mind which has a kind of sensibility, of subtle contact with the psychic being, is capable of feeling the presence of the soul in others.

Those who have the ability to enter to a certain extent into the consciousness of others to the point of being able to see or feel directly their thought, their mental activity, who can enter the mental atmosphere of others without needing to use words to make themselves understood, can easily differentiate between someone whose soul is active and someone whose soul is asleep. The activity of the soul gives a special colouring to the mental activity — it is lighter, more comprehensive and luminous — so that can be felt. For instance, by looking into someone's eyes you can say with some certainty that this person has a living soul or that you don't see his soul in his eyes. Many people can feel — "many", I mean among evolved people — can say that. But naturally, to know exactly how far somebody's soul is awake and active, how far it rules the being, is the master, one must have the psychic consciousness oneself, for that alone can judge definitively. But it is not altogether impossible to have that sort of inner vibration which makes you say, "Oh! This person has a soul."

Now, obviously, most often what people — unless they are initiated — call "soul" is the vital activity. If someone has a strong, active, obstinate vital which rules the body's activities, which has a very living or intense contact with people and things and events, if he has a marked taste for art, for all expressions of beauty, we are generally tempted to say and believe, "Oh! He has a living soul"; but it is not his soul, it is his vital being which is alive and dominates the activities of the body. That is the first difference between someone who is beginning to be developed and those who are still in the inertia and *tamas* of the purely material life. This gives, first to the appearance and also to the activity, a kind of vibration, of intensity of vibration, which often creates the impression that this person has a living soul; but it is not that, it is his vital which is developed, which has a special capacity, is stronger than the physical inertia and gives an intensity of vibration and life and action that those whose vital being is not developed do not possess. This confusion between the vital activity and the soul is a very frequent one.... The vital vibration is much more easily perceptible to the human consciousness than the vibration of the soul.

To perceive the soul in someone, as a rule the mind must be very quiet — very quiet, for when it is active, *its* vibrations are seen, not the vibration of the soul.

And then, when you look at someone who is conscious of his soul, and lives in his soul, if you look like this, the impression you have is of descending, of entering deep, deep, deep into the person, far, far, far, far within; while usually when you look into someone's eyes, you very soon come to a surface which vibrates and answers your look, but you don't have that feeling of going down, down, down, down, going deep as into a hole and very far, very, very, very far within, so you have... a small, very quiet response. Otherwise, usually you enter — there are eyes you cannot enter, they are closed like a door; but still there are eyes which are open — you enter and then, quite close behind, you come to something vibrating there, like this, shining at times, vibrating. And then, that's it; if you make a mistake, you say, "Oh! He has a living soul" — it is not that, it is his vital.

In order to find the soul you must go in this way (*gesture of going deep within*), like this, draw back from the surface, withdraw deep within and enter, enter, enter, go down, down, down into a very deep hole, silent, immobile, and there, there's a kind of... something warm, quiet, rich in substance and very still, and very full, like a sweetness — that is the soul.

And if one is insistent and is conscious oneself, then there comes a kind of plenitude which gives the feeling of something complete that contains unfathomable depths in which, should one enter, one feels that many secrets would be revealed... like the reflection in very peaceful waters of something that is eternal. And one no longer feels limited by time.

One has the feeling of having always been and of being for eternity.

That is when one has touched the core of the soul.

And if the contact has been conscious and complete enough, it liberates you from the bondage of outer form; you no longer feel that you live only because you have a body. That is usually the ordinary sensation of the being, to be so tied to this outer form that when one thinks of "myself" one thinks of the body. That is the usual thing. The personal reality is the body's reality. It is only when one has made an effort for inner development and tried to find something that is a little more stable in one's being, that one can begin to feel that this "something" which is permanently conscious throughout all ages and all change, this something must be "myself". But that already requires a study that is rather deep. Otherwise if you think "I am going to do this", "I need that", it is always your body, a small kind of will which is a mixture of sensations, of more or less confused sentimental reactions, and still more confused thoughts which form a mixture and are animated by an impulse, an attraction, a desire, some sort of a will; and all that momentarily becomes "myself" — but not directly, for one does not conceive this "myself" as independent of the head, the trunk, the arms and legs and all that moves — it is very closely linked.

It is only after having thought much, seen much, studied

much, observed much that you begin to realise that the one is more or less independent of the other and that the will behind can make it either act or not act, and you begin not to be completely identified with the movement, the action, the realisation — that something is floating. But you have to observe much to see that.

And then you must observe much more still to see that this, the second thing that is there, this kind of active conscious will, is set in motion by "something else" which watches, judges, decides and tries to found its decisions on knowledge — that happens even much later. And so, when you begin to see this "something else", you begin to see that it has the power to set in motion the second thing, which is an active will; and not only that, but that it has a very direct and very important action on the reactions, the feelings, the sensations, and that finally it can have control over all the movements of the being — this part which watches, observes, judges and decides.

That is the beginning of control.

When one becomes conscious of that, one has seized the thread, and when one speaks of control, one can know, "Ah! Yes, this is what has the power of control."

This is how one learns to look at oneself.[171]

Knowing What the Soul Knows

"What the soul sees and has experienced, that it knows; the rest is appearance, prejudice and opinion."

Sri Aurobindo, *Thoughts and Aphorisms*

This amounts to saying that all knowledge which is not the result of the soul's vision or experience is without true value.

But the question immediately arises — it was, in fact, put to me — "How do we know what the soul sees?"

Obviously there is only one solution: to become conscious of one's soul. And this completes the aphorism: unless one is conscious of one's soul one does not have true knowledge. Therefore the first effort must be to find the soul within, to unite with it and allow it to govern one's life.

Some people ask, "How do we know whether this is the soul?" I have already answered this question several times. Those who ask this question, by the very fact of asking it, prove that they are not conscious of their souls, because as soon as you are conscious of your soul and identified with it, you have a positive knowledge of it and you no longer ask how you are to know. And that experience can neither be counterfeited nor imagined; you cannot pretend to be in contact with your soul — it is something which cannot be contrived or counterfeited. When the soul governs your life, you know it with absolute certainty and no longer ask any questions.

But the usefulness of the aphorism we have just read is to make you understand that everything you think you know, everything you have learnt, anything that has come to you in your life through personal observation, deduction, comparison — all that is a very relative knowledge on which you cannot found a durable and truly effective way of life.

How many times have we repeated this: all that comes from the mind is wholly relative. The more the mind is educated and has applied itself to various disciplines, the more it becomes capable of proving that what it puts forward or what

it says is true. One can prove the truth of anything by reasoning, but that does not make it true. It remains an opinion, a
prejudice, a knowledge based on appearances which are themselves more than dubious.

So there seems to be only one way out and that is to go in
search of one's soul and to find it. It is there, it does not make
a point of hiding itself, it does not play with you just to make
things difficult; on the contrary, it makes great efforts to help
you find it and to make itself heard. Only, between your soul
and your active consciousness there are two characters who
are in the habit of making a lot of noise, the mind and the
vital. And because they make a lot of noise, while the soul
does not, or, rather, makes as little as possible, their noise
prevents you from hearing the voice of the soul.

When you want to know what your soul knows, you have
to make an inner effort, to be very attentive; and indeed, if you
are attentive, behind the outer noise of the mind and the vital,
you can discern something very subtle, very quiet, very peaceful, which knows and says what it knows. But the insistence of
the others is so imperious, while *that* is so quiet, that you are
very easily misled into listening to the one that makes the most
noise; most often you become aware only afterwards that the
other one was right. It does not impose itself, it does not compel you to listen, for it is without violence.

When you hesitate, when you wonder what to do in this
or that circumstance, there come the desire, the preference
both mental and vital, that press, insist, affirm and impose
themselves, and, with the best reasons in the world, build up
a whole case for themselves. And if you are not on the alert,
if you don't have a firm discipline, if you don't have the habit

of control, they finally convince you that they are right. And as I was saying a little while ago, they make so much noise that you do not even hear the tiny voice or the tiny, very quiet indication of the soul which says, "Don't do it."

This "Don't do it" comes often, but you discard it as something which has no power and follow your impulsive destiny. But if you are truly sincere in your will to find and live the truth, then you learn to listen better and better, you learn to discriminate more and more, and even if it costs you an effort, even if it causes you pain, you learn to obey. And even if you have obeyed only once, it is a powerful help, a considerable progress on the path towards the discrimination between what is and what is not the soul. With this discrimination and the necessary sincerity you are sure to reach the goal.

But you must not be in a hurry, you must not be impatient, you must be very persevering. You do the wrong thing ten times for every time that you do the right thing. But when you do the wrong thing you must not give up everything in despair, but tell yourself that the Grace will never abandon you and that next time it will be better.

So, in conclusion, we shall say that in order to know things as they are you must first unite with your soul and to unite with your soul you must want it with persistence and perseverance.

Only the degree of concentration on the goal can shorten the way.[172]

Intuition and Its Development

Mother, how can the faculty of intuition be developed?

There are different kinds of intuition, and we carry these capacities within us. They are always active to some extent but we don't notice them because we don't pay enough attention to what is going on in us.

Behind the emotions, deep within the being, in a consciousness seated somewhere near the level of the solar plexus, there is a sort of prescience, a kind of capacity for foresight, but not in the form of ideas: rather in the form of feelings, almost a perception of sensations. For instance, when one is going to decide to do something, there is sometimes a kind of uneasiness or inner refusal, and usually, if one listens to this deeper indication, one realises that it was justified.

In other cases there is something that urges, indicates, insists — I am not speaking of impulses, you understand, of all the movements which come from the vital and much lower still — indications which are behind the feelings, which come from the affective part of the being; there too one can receive a fairly sure indication of the thing to be done. These are forms of intuition or of a higher instinct which can be cultivated by observation and also by studying the results. Naturally, it must be done very sincerely, objectively, without prejudice. If one wants to see things in a particular way and at the same time practise this observation, it is all useless. One must do it as if one were looking at what is happening from outside oneself, in someone else.

It is one form of intuition and perhaps the first one that usually manifests.

There is also another form but that one is much more difficult to observe because for those who are accustomed to think, to act by reason — not by impulse but by reason — to reflect before doing anything, there is an extremely swift process from cause to effect in the half-conscious thought which prevents you from seeing the line, the whole line of reasoning and so you don't think that it is a chain of reasoning, and that is quite deceptive. You have the impression of an intuition but it is not an intuition, it is an extremely rapid subconscious reasoning, which takes up a problem and goes straight to the conclusions. This must not be mistaken for intuition.

In the ordinary functioning of the brain, intuition is something which suddenly falls like a drop of light. If one has the faculty, the beginning of a faculty of mental vision, it gives the impression of something coming from outside or above, like a little impact of a drop of light in the brain, absolutely independent of all reasoning.

This is perceived more easily when one is able to silence one's mind, hold it still and attentive, arresting its usual functioning, as if the mind were changed into a kind of mirror turned towards a higher faculty in a sustained and silent attention. That too one can learn to do. One *must* learn to do it, it is a necessary discipline.

When you have a question to solve, whatever it may be, usually you concentrate your attention here (*pointing between the eyebrows*), at the centre just above the eyes, the centre of the conscious will. But then if you do that, you cannot be in

contact with intuition. You can be in contact with the source
of the will, of effort, even of a certain kind of knowledge, but
in the outer, almost material field; whereas, if you want to
contact the intuition, you must keep this (*Mother indicates
the forehead*) completely immobile. Active thought must be
stopped as far as possible and the entire mental faculty must
form — at the top of the head and a little further above if
possible — a kind of mirror, very quiet, very still, turned
upwards, in silent, very concentrated attention. If you succeed, you can — perhaps not immediately — but you can
have the perception of the drops of light falling upon the
mirror from a still unknown region and expressing themselves
as a conscious thought which has no connection with all the
rest of your thought since you have been able to keep it silent. That is the real beginning of the intellectual intuition.

It is a discipline to be followed. For a long time one may
try and not succeed, but as soon as one succeeds in making a
"mirror", still and attentive, one always obtains a result, not
necessarily with a precise form of thought but always with
the sensations of a light coming from above. And then, if one
can receive this light coming from above without entering
immediately into a whirl of activity, receive it in calm and
silence and let it penetrate deep into the being, then after a
while it expresses itself either as a luminous thought or as a
very precise indication here (*Mother indicates the heart*), in
this other centre.

Naturally, first these two faculties must be developed; then,
as soon as there is any result, one must observe the result, as
I said, and see the connection with what is happening, the
consequences: see, observe very attentively what has come

in, what may have caused a distortion, what one has added by way of more or less conscious reasoning or the intervention of a lower will, also more or less conscious; and it is by a very deep study — indeed, almost of every moment, in any case daily and very frequent — that one succeeds in developing one's intuition. It takes a long time. It takes a long time and there are ambushes: one can deceive oneself, take for intuitions subconscious wills which try to manifest, indications given by impulses one has refused to receive openly, indeed all sorts of difficulties. One must be prepared for that. But if one persists, one is sure to succeed.

And there comes a time when one feels a kind of inner guidance, something which is leading one very perceptibly in all that one does. But then, for the guidance to have its maximum power, one must naturally add to it a conscious surrender: one must be sincerely determined to follow the indication given by the higher force. If one does that, then... one saves years of study, one can seize the result extremely rapidly. If one also does that, the result comes very rapidly. But for that, it must be done with sincerity and... a kind of inner spontaneity. If one wants to try without this surrender, one may succeed — as one can also succeed in developing one's personal will and making it into a very considerable power — but that takes a very long time and one meets many obstacles and the result is very precarious; one must be very persistent, obstinate, persevering, and one is sure to succeed, but only after a great labour.[173]

Sincerity and Division in the Being

> "To be absolutely sincere is not to have any division, any
> contradiction in one's being."   — The Mother

If you are made of pieces which are not only different but
often quite contradictory, these pieces necessarily create a
division in your being. For example, you have one part in
yourself which aspires for the divine life, to know the Divine, to unite with Him, to live Him integrally, and then you
have another part which has attachments, desires — which
it calls "needs" — and which not only seeks these things but
is quite upset when it does not have them. There are other
contradictions, but this one is the most flagrant. There are
others, for instance, like wanting to surrender completely to
the Divine, to give oneself up totally to His Will and His
Guidance, and at the same time, when the experience comes
— a common experience on the path when one sincerely
tries to give oneself up to the Divine — the feeling that one
is nothing, that one can do nothing, that one doesn't even
exist outside the Divine; that is to say, if He were not there,
one would not exist and could not do anything, one would
not be anything at all.... This experience naturally comes as
a help on the path of total self-giving, but there is a part of
the being which, when the experience comes, rises up in a
terrible revolt and says, "But, excuse me! I insist on existing, I insist on being something, I insist on doing things
myself, I want to have a personality." And naturally, the second one undoes all that the first had done.

These are not exceptional cases, this happens very frequently. I could give you innumerable examples of such contradictions in the being: when one part tries to take a step forward, the other one comes and demolishes everything. So you have to begin again all the time, and every time it is demolished. That is why you must do this work of sincerity which, when you perceive in your being a part that pulls the other way, makes you take it up carefully, educate it as one educates a child and put it in harmony with the central part. That is the work of sincerity and it is indispensable.

And naturally, when there is a unity, an agreement, a harmony among all the wills of the being, your being can become simple, candid and uniform in its action and tendencies. It is only when the whole being is grouped around a single central movement that you can be spontaneous. For if, within you, there is something which is turned towards the Divine and awaits the inspiration and impulse, and at the same time there is another part of the being which seeks its own ends and works to realise its own desires, you no longer know where you stand, and you can no longer be sure of what may happen, for one part can not only undo but totally contradict what the other wants to do.[174]

Spontaneity

What Lao Tse calls spontaneous is this: instead of being moved by a personal will — mental, vital or physical — one ought to stop all outer effort and let oneself be guided and moved by what the Chinese call *Tao*, which they identify with the Godhead — or God or the Supreme Principle or the

Origin of all things or the creative Truth, indeed all possible human notions of the Divine and the goal to be attained.

To be spontaneous means not to think out, organise, decide and make an effort to realise with the personal will.

... Naturally, this is not very easy, it asks for preparation.

And if one comes down to the sphere of action, it is still more difficult; for normally, if one wants to act with some kind of logic, one usually has to think out beforehand what one wants to do and plan it before doing it, otherwise one may be tossed about by all sorts of desires and impulses which would be very far from the inspiration spoken about in *Wu Wei*; it would simply be movements of the lower nature driving you to act. Therefore, unless one has reached the state of wisdom and detachment of the Chinese sage mentioned in this story, it is better not to be spontaneous in one's daily actions, for one would risk being the plaything of all the most disorderly impulses and influences.[175]

*

"I saw a child wallowing in the dirt and the same child cleaned by his mother and resplendent, but each time I trembled before his utter purity."

                                    Sri Aurobindo, *Thoughts and Aphorisms*

Can a child keep this purity even when he has grown up?

In theory, it is not impossible, and some people born away from cities, civilisations and cultures may maintain throughout the life of their earthly body this spontaneous purity, a purity of the soul that is not obscured by the mind's working.

For the purity of which Sri Aurobindo speaks here is the purity of instinct, that obeys Nature's impulses spontaneously, never calculating, never questioning, never asking whether it is good or bad, whether what one does is right or wrong, whether it is a virtue or a sin, whether the outcome will be favourable or unfavourable. All these notions come into play when the mental ego makes its appearance and begins to take a dominant position in the consciousness and to veil the spontaneity of the soul.

In modern "civilised" life, parents and teachers, by their practical and rational "good advice", lose no time in covering up this spontaneity which they call unconsciousness, and substituting for it a very small, very narrow, limited mental ego, withdrawn into itself, crammed with notions of misbehaviour and sin and punishment or of personal interest, calculation and profit; all of which has the inevitable result of increasing vital desires through repression, fear or self-justification.

And yet for the sake of completeness it should be added that because man is a mental being, he must necessarily in the course of his evolution leave behind this unconscious and spontaneous purity, which is very similar to the purity of the animal, and after passing through an unavoidable period of mental perversion and impurity, rise beyond the mind into the higher and luminous purity of the divine consciousness.[176]

*

Does spontaneity come spontaneously or does one have to follow a discipline to obtain it?

Spontaneity in feelings and action comes from a permanent contact with the psychic, which brings order into the thoughts and automatically controls the vital impulses.[177]

How to Will

Sweet Mother, how can we make our resolution very firm?

By wanting it to be very firm! (*Laughter*)

No, this seems like a joke... but it is absolutely true. One does not want it truly. There is always, if you... It is a lack of sincerity. If you look sincerely, you will see that you have decided that it will be like this, and then, beneath there is something which has not decided at all and is waiting for the second of hesitation in order to rush forward. If you are sincere, if you are sincere and get hold of the part which is hiding, waiting, not showing itself, which knows that there will come a second of indecision when it can rush out and make you do the thing you have decided not to do...

But if you *really* want it, *nothing* in the world can prevent you from doing what you want. It is because one doesn't know how to will it. It is because one is *divided* in one's will. If you are not divided in your will, I say that nothing, nobody in the world can make you change your will.

But one doesn't know how to will it. In fact one doesn't

even want to. These are velleities: "Well, it is like this.... It would be good if it were like that... yes, it would be better if it were like that... yes, it would be preferable if it were like that." But *this* is not to will. And always there at the back, hidden somewhere in a corner of the brain, is something which is looking on and saying, "Oh, why should I want that? After all one can as well want the opposite." And to try, you see... Not like that, just wait... But one can always find a thousand excuses to do the opposite. And ah, just a tiny little wavering is enough... pftt... the thing swoops down and there it is. But if one *wills*, if one really *knows* that *this* is the thing, and truly wants this, and if one is *oneself* entirely concentrated in the will, I say that there is *nothing* in the world that can prevent one from doing it, from doing it or being obliged to do it. It depends on what it is.

One wants. Yes, one wants, like this (*gestures*). One wants: "Yes, yes, it would be better if it were like that. Yes, it would be finer also, more elegant."... But, eh, eh, after all one is a weak creature, isn't that so? And then one can always put the blame upon something else: "It is the influence coming from outside, it is all kinds of circumstances."

The breath has passed, you see. You don't know... something... a moment of unconsciousness... "Oh, I was not conscious." You are not conscious because you do not accept... And all this because one doesn't know how to will.

To learn how to will is a very important thing. And to will truly, you must unify your being. In fact, to be a being, one must first unify oneself. If one is pulled by absolutely opposite tendencies, if one spends three-fourths of his life without being conscious of himself and the reasons why he does things, is one a real being? One does not exist. One is a mass of influences, movements, forces, actions, reactions, but one is not a being. One begins to become a being when he begins to have a will. And one can't have a will unless he is unified.

And when you have a will, you will be able to say, say to the Divine: "I want what You want." But not before that. Because in order to want what the Divine wants, you must have a will, otherwise you can will nothing at all. You would like to. You would like it very much. You would very much like to want what the Divine wants to do. You don't possess a will to give to Him and to put at His service. Something like that, gelatinous, like jelly-fish... there... a mass of good wills — and I am considering the better side of things and forgetting the bad wills — a mass of good wills, half-conscious and fluctuating.[178]

Mental Honesty

It would seem that in the ordinary psychological constitution of man, the almost constant function of the mind is to give an acceptable explanation of what goes on in the "desire-being", the vital, the most material parts of the mind and the subtlest parts of the body. There is a kind of general complicity in all the parts of the being to give an explanation and even a comfortable justification for everything we do, in order to avoid as far as possible the painful impressions left by the mistakes we commit and undesirable movements. For instance, unless one has undergone or taken up a special training, whatever one does, the mind gives itself a favourable enough explanation of it, so that one is not troubled. Only under the pressure of outer reactions or circumstances or movements coming from other people, does one gradually consent to look less favourably at what one is and does, and begins to ask oneself whether things could not be better than they are.

Spontaneously, the first movement is what is known as self-defense. One puts oneself on one's guard and quite spontaneously one wants a justification... for the smallest things, absolutely insignificant things — it is a normal attitude in life.

And explanations — one gives them to oneself; it is only under the pressure of circumstances that one begins to give them to others or to another, but first one makes oneself very comfortable; first thing: "It was like that, for it had to be like that, and it happened because of this, and...", and it is always the fault of circumstances or other people. And it truly requires an effort — unless, as I say, one has undergone a discipline, has acquired the habit of doing it automatically — it requires an effort to begin to understand that perhaps things are not like this, that perhaps one has not done exactly what one ought to have done or reacted as one should. And even when one begins to see it, a much greater effort is needed to recognise it... officially.

When one begins to see that one has made a mistake, the first movement of the mind is to push it into the background and to put a cloak in front of it, the cloak of a very fine little explanation, and as long as one is not obliged to show it, one hides it. And this is what I call "lack of mental honesty".

First, one deceives oneself by habit, but even when one begins not to deceive oneself, instinctively there is a movement of trying, trying to deceive oneself in order to feel comfortable. And so a still greater step is necessary once one has understood that one was deceiving oneself, to confess frankly, "Yes, I was deceiving myself."

All these things are so habitual, so automatic, as it were, that you are not even aware of them; but when you begin to want to establish some discipline over your being, you make discoveries which are really tremendously interesting. When you have discovered this, you become aware that you are living constantly in a... the best word is "self-deception", a state of wilful deceit; that is, you deceive yourself spontaneously. It is not that you need to reflect: spontaneously you put a pretty cloak over what you have done so that it doesn't show its true colours... and all this for things which are so insignificant, which have so little importance! It would be understandable, wouldn't it, if recognising your mistake had serious consequences for your very existence — the instinct of self-preservation would make you do it as a protection — but that is not the question, it concerns things which are absolutely unimportant, of no consequence at all except that of having to tell yourself, "I have made a mistake."

This means that an effort is needed in order to be mentally sincere. There must be an effort, there must be a discipline. Of course, I am not speaking of those who tell lies in order not to be caught, for everybody knows that this should not be done. Besides, the most stupid lies are the most useless, for they are so flagrant that they can't deceive anyone. Such examples occur constantly; you catch someone doing something wrong and tell him, "That's how it is"; he gives a silly explanation which nobody can understand, nobody can accept; it is silly but he gives it in the hope of shielding himself. It is spontaneous, you see, but he knows this is not done. But the other kind of deception is much more spontaneous and it is so habitual that one is not aware of it. So, when we speak of mental honesty, we speak of something which is acquired by a very constant and sustained effort.

You catch yourself, don't you, you suddenly catch yourself in the act of giving yourself somewhere in your head or here (*Mother indicates the heart*), here it is more serious... giving a very favourable little explanation. And only when you can get a grip on yourself, there, hold fast and look at yourself clearly in the face and say, "Do you think it is like that?", then, if you are very courageous and put a very strong pressure, in the end you tell yourself, "Yes, I know very well that it is not like that!"

It sometimes takes years. Time must pass, one must have changed much within oneself, one's vision of things must have become different, one must be in a different condition, in a different relation with circumstances, in order to see clearly, completely, how far one was deceiving oneself — and at that moment one was convinced that one was sincere.[179]

Two Ways of Self-Deception

"When I hear of a righteous wrath, I wonder at man's capacity for self-deception."

Sri Aurobindo, *Thoughts and Aphorisms*

... actually there are two ways of deceiving oneself, which

are very different. For example, you may very well be shocked by certain things, not for personal reasons, but precisely in your goodwill and eagerness to serve the Divine, when you see people behaving badly, being selfish, unfaithful and treacherous. There is a stage where you have overcome these things and no longer allow them to manifest in yourself, but to the extent that you are linked to the ordinary consciousness, the ordinary point of view, the ordinary life, the ordinary way of thinking, they are still possible, they exist latently because they are the reverse of the qualities that you are striving to attain. And this opposition still exists — until you rise above it and no longer have either the quality or the defect. So long as you have the virtue, its opposite is always latent in you; it is only when you are above both the virtue and the defect that it disappears.

So this kind of indignation that you feel comes from the fact that you are not altogether above it; you are at the stage where you thoroughly disapprove and could not do it yourself. Up to that point there is nothing to say, unless you give a violent outer expression to your indignation. If anger intervenes, it is because there is a complete contradiction between the feeling you want to have and how you react to others. Because anger is a deformation of the vital power, an obscure and wholly unregenerated vital, a vital that is still subject to all the ordinary actions and reactions. When this vital power is used by an ignorant and egoistic individual will and this will meets with opposition from other individual wills around it, this power, under the pressure of opposition, changes into anger and tries to obtain by violence what cannot be achieved solely by the pressure of the force itself.

Besides, anger, like every other kind of violence, is always a sign of weakness, impotence and incapacity.

And here self-deception comes solely from the approval given to it or the flattering epithet attached to it — because anger can only be something blind, ignorant and asuric, that is to say, contrary to the light.

But this is still the best case.

There is another one. There are people who without knowing it — or because *they want* to ignore it — always follow their personal interest, their preferences, their attachments, their conceptions; people who are not wholly consecrated to the Divine and who make use of moral and yogic ideas to conceal their personal impulses. But these people are deceiving themselves doubly; not only do they deceive themselves in their external activities, in their relation with others, but they also deceive themselves in their own personal movement; instead of serving the Divine, they serve their own egoism. And this happens constantly, constantly! They serve their own personality, their own egoism, while pretending to serve God. Then it is no longer even self-deception, it is hypocrisy.

This mental habit of always endowing everything with a very favourable appearance, of giving a favourable explanation to all movements — sometimes it is rather subtle, but sometimes it is so crude that nobody is deceived except oneself. It is a habit of excusing oneself, the habit of giving a favourable mental excuse, a favourable mental explanation to everything one does, to everything one says, to everything one feels. For example, those who have no self-control and slap someone's face in great indignation would call that an almost divine wrath!

It is amazing, amazing — this power of self-deception, the mind's skill in finding an admirable justification for any ignorance, any stupidity whatsoever.

This is not an experience that comes only now and then. It is something which you can observe from minute to minute. And you usually see it much more easily in others! But if you look at yourself closely, you catch yourself a thousand times a day, looking at yourself just a little indulgently: "Oh! But it is *not the same thing*." Besides, it is never the same for you as it is for your neighbour![180]

Reviewing the Movements of One's Being

One must be clearly aware of the origin of one's movements because there are contradictory velleities in the being — some pushing you here, others pushing you there, and that obviously creates a chaos in life. If you observe yourself, you will see that as soon as you do something which disturbs you a little, the mind immediately gives you a favourable reason to justify yourself — this mind is capable of gilding everything. In these conditions it is difficult to know oneself. One must be absolutely sincere to be able to do it and to see clearly into all the little falsehoods of the mental being.

If in your mind you go over the various movements and reactions of the day like one repeating indefinitely the same thing, you will not progress. If this reviewing is to make you progress, you must find something within you in whose light you can be yourself your own judge, something which represents for you the best part of yourself, which has some light, some goodwill and which precisely is in love with progress. Place that before you and first, pass across it as in a cinema all that you have done, all that you have felt, your impulses, your thoughts, etc.; then try to coordinate them, that is, find out why this has followed that. And look at the luminous screen that is before you: certain things pass by well, without throwing a shadow; others, on the contrary, throw a little shadow; others yet cast a shadow altogether black and disagreeable. You must do this very sincerely, as though you were playing a game: under such circumstances I did such and such a thing, feeling like this and thinking in this way; I have before me my ideal of knowledge and self-mastery, well, was this act in keeping with my ideal or not? If it was, it would not leave any shadow on the screen, which would remain transparent, and one would not have to worrry about it. If it is not in conformity, it casts a shadow. Why has it left this shadow? What was there in this act that was contrary to the the will to self-knowledge and self-mastery? Most often you will find that it corresponds to unconsciousness — then you file it among unconscious things and resolve that next time you will try to be conscious before doing anything. But in other cases you will see that it was a nasty little egoism, quite black, which had come to distort your action or your thought. Then you place this egoism before your "light" and ask yourself: "Why has it the right to make me act like that, think like that?"... And instead of accepting any odd explanation you must search and you will find in a corner of your being something which thinks and says, "Ah, no, I shall accept everything but that." You will see that it is a petty vanity, a movement of self-love, an egoistic feeling hidden somewhere, a hundred things. Then you take a good look at these things in the light of your ideal: "Is cherishing this movement in conformity with my seeking and the realisation of my ideal or not? I put this little dark corner in front of the light until the light enters into it and it disappears." Then the comedy is over. But the comedy of your whole day is not finished yet, you know, for there are many things which have to pass thus before the light. But if you continue this game — for truly it is a game, if you do this sincerely — I assure you that in six months you will not recognise yourself, you will say to yourself, "What? I was like that! It is impossible!"

You may be five years old or twenty, fifty or sixty and yet transform yourself in this way by putting everything before this inner light. You will see that the elements which do not conform with your ideal are not generally elements which you have to throw wholly out of yourself (there are very few of this kind); they are simply things not in their place. If you organise everything — your feelings, your thoughts, your impulses, etc. — around the psychic centre which is the inner light, you will see that all inner disorder will change into a luminous order.[181]

Pleasure and Joy

> *Sweet Mother, sometimes when one feels depressed it lasts quite a long time; but when one feels a special kind of joy, it does not last.*

Yes, that is very true.

Then what should one do to make it last longer?

But it is not the same part of the being that has the depression and the joy.

If you are speaking of pleasure, the pleasure of the vital is something very fleeting, and I think that in life — in life as it is at present — there are more occasions for displeasure than for pleasure. Pleasure in itself is extremely fleeting, for if the same vibration of pleasure is prolonged a little, it becomes unpleasant or even repulsive — exactly the same vibration.

Pleasure in itself is something very fugitive. But if you are speaking of joy, that is something altogether different, it is a kind of warmth and illumination in the heart, you see — one may feel joy in the mind also, but it is a kind of warmth and beatific illumination occurring somewhere. That is a quality which is not yet fully developed and one is rarely in the psychological state that's needed to have it. And that is why it is fugitive. Otherwise joy is constantly there in the truth of the being, in the reality of the being, in your true Self, in your soul, in your psychic being, joy is constantly there.

It has nothing to do with pleasure: it is a kind of inner delight.

But one is rarely in a state to feel it, unless one has become fully conscious of one's psychic being. That is why when it comes it is fugitive, for the psychological condition necessary to perceive it is not often there. On the other hand, one is almost constantly in an ordinary vital state where the least unpleasant thing very spontaneously and easily brings you depression — depression if you are a weak person, revolt if you are a strong one. Every desire which is not satisfied, every impulse which meets an obstacle, every unpleasant contact with outside things, very easily and very spontaneously creates depression or revolt, for that is the normal state of things — normal in life as it is today. While joy is an exceptional state.

And so, pleasure, pleasure which is simply a pleasing sensation — if it lasts, not only does it lose its edge, but it ends up by becoming unpleasant; one can't bear it long. So, quite naturally it comes and goes. That is to say, the very thing that gives you pleasure — exactly the same vibration — after a short while, doesn't give it to you any longer. And if it persists, it becomes unpleasant for you. That is why you can't have pleasure for a long time.

The only thing which can be lasting is joy, if one enters into contact with the truth of the being which holds this joy permanently.[182]

The Substance of the Psychic

What characterises the substance of the psychic world?

The substance of the psychic world is a substance proper to it, with its own psychic characteristics: a sense of immortality, a complete receptivity to the divine influence, an entire submission to this influence by which it is wholly impregnated. It is this exactly which distinguishes the psychic from the other parts of the being. When, for instance, I speak of organising the mind and the vital around the psychic centre,

I do not mean that they become psychic; they remain the mind and the vital, but they are organised around the psychic as an army is organised around its leader — it does not become the leader, it obeys him, doesn't it? Well, it is the same thing here; the vital and the mind are organised around the psychic, they receive orders from the psychic and carry them out as well as they can. But their substance does not become psychic substance as a consequence. They can be under the influence of the psychic and assume its nature more or less but not its substance.[183]

Difference between "Spiritual" and "Psychic"

What is the difference between "spiritual" and "psychic"?

It is not the same thing. The psychic is the being organised by the divine Presence and it belongs to the earth — I am not speaking of the universe, only of the earth; it is only upon earth that you will find the psychic being. The rest of the universe is formed in quite a different way.

The universe contains all the domains higher than the physical: there is a global physical comprising the mental, the vital, etc., and all the domains above the mental are domains of a spiritual order, domains which are, for us, domains of the spirit, and it is this "spirit" which little by little, progressively, materialises itself to arrive at Matter as we conceive it. The beings of the Overmind, for instance, and all the beings of the higher regions have no psychic being —

the "angels" have no psychic being. It is only upon earth that
the psychic life begins, and it is just the process by which the
Divine has awakened material life to the necessity of rejoin-
ing its divine origin. Without the psychic, Matter would never
have awakened from its inconscience, it would never have
aspired for the life of its origin, the spiritual life. Therefore,
the psychic being in the human being is the manifestation of
spiritual aspiration; but there is a spiritual life independent
of the psychic.[184]

What Aspires in Everybody

> "Our one objective must be the Divine himself to whom,
> knowingly or unknowingly, something always aspires in
> our secret nature."   — Sri Aurobindo, *The Synthesis of Yoga*

What is this something which aspires, Sweet Mother?

It is a part of the being which is not always the same in everyone, and which is instinctively open to the influence of the
psychic.

There is always one part — sometimes indeed quite veiled,
of which we are not conscious — something in the being
which is turned to the psychic and receiving its influence.
This is the intermediary between the psychic consciousness
and the external consciousness.

It is not the same thing in everyone; in each one it is
different. It is the point in his nature or character through
which he can touch the psychic and where he can receive the

psychic influence. It depends upon people; for each one it is different; everyone has a point like this.

You may also feel that there are certain things which suddenly push you, lift you above yourself, open a kind of door upon something greater. It can be many things; and it depends upon each one's nature. It's the part of the being which enthuses over something; it is this capacity for enthusiasm.

There are two principal things. This, the capacity for enthusiasm which makes one come out of his greater or lesser inertia in order to throw himself more or less totally into the thing which rouses him. As for instance, the artist for his art, the scientist for his science. And in general, every person who creates or builds has an opening, the opening of a special faculty, a special possibility, creating an enthusiasm in him. When this is active, something in the being awakens, and there is a participation of almost the whole being in the thing done.

There is this. And then there are those who have an innate faculty of gratitude, those who have an ardent need to respond, respond with warmth, devotion, joy, to something which they feel like a marvel hidden behind the whole of life, behind the tiniest little element, the least little event of life, who feel this sovereign beauty or infinite Grace which is behind all things.

I knew people who had no knowledge, so to say, of anything, who were hardly educated, whose minds were altogether of the ordinary kind, and who had in them this capacity of gratitude, of warmth, which gives itself, understands and is thankful.

Well, for them, the contact with the psychic was very

frequent, almost constant and, to the extent that they were capable of it, conscious — not very conscious but a little — in the sense that they felt that they were carried, helped, uplifted above themselves.

These two things prepare people the most. They are born with one or the other; and if they take the trouble, it develops gradually, it increases.

We say: the capacity for enthusiasm, something which throws you out of your miserable and mean little ego; and the generous gratitude, the generosity of the gratitude which also flings itself in thanksgiving out of the little ego. These are the two most powerful levers to enter into contact with the Divine in one's psychic being. This serves as a link with the psychic being — the surest link.

(Silence)

That's all?

> *Sweet Mother, does something aspire even in the most nasty people?*

In the most nasty people?... yes, my child — even in the Asuras, even in the Adversaries, even in the monsters, there is something.

There is always a corner, a kind of rift, a sensitive point, which is usually called a weakness. But this actually is the strength of the being, the point by which it can be touched.

For even in the most obscure and misled beings, even in those whose conscious will is to fight against the Divine, in spite of themselves, in spite of everything, their origin is divine. And they work in vain, try in vain to cut themselves off from their origin; they cannot do it. Deliberately, consciously, they try all they can; but they know very well they cannot do it. Even the most monstrous being there is always a means to touch.[185]

Does Everyone Always Progress?

Sweet Mother, do those who have this aspiration without knowing it also progress without knowing it?

Yes — yes.

Then everybody is progressing, always, isn't that so?

In a certain way, yes. Only it may not be apparent in one lifetime, because when there is no conscious participation of the being, the movement is relatively slow, even relative to the short duration of human life. And so it is quite possible, for example, that at the moment of death a being seems not to have progressed, and even sometimes it seems to have been going backwards, to have lost what it had at the beginning of its life. But if we take the great life-curve of its psychic being through many lives, there is always a progress. Each experience it had in one of its physical lifetimes helps it to make some progress. But it is the psychic being which always progresses.

The physical being, in the state in which it is at present — well, having reached a certain point of ascent, it comes down again. There are elements which may not come down again grossly; but still it does come down, one can't deny it.

The vital being — not necessarily, nor the mental being. The vital being, if it knows how to get connected with the universal force, can very easily have no retrogression; it can continue to ascend. And the mental being, it's absolutely certain, is completely free from all degeneration if it continues to develop normally. So these always make progress so long as they remain co-ordinated and under the influence of the psychic.

It is only the physical being which grows and decomposes. But this comes from its lack of plasticity and receptivity and by its very nature; it is not inevitable. Therefore there is room to think that at a given moment, as the physical consciousness itself progresses consciously and deliberately, well, to a certain extent and increasingly the body itself will be able, first to resist decay — which, obviously, must be the first movement — and then gradually begin to grow in inner perfection till it overcomes the forces of decomposition.

But truly speaking, it's the only thing which for the moment does not progress. Everything else is progressing.

But this substance *itself* — that is, this material physical substance which forms it constitutes an organism which lives for a certain length of time in a given form and then this form declines and dissolves — the substance itself constituting these successive forms progresses through all these forms. That is, the molecular, cellular substance — perhaps even the cellular — the molecular and atomic, is progressing in its capacity to express the divine Force and Consciousness. Through all these organisms this substance becomes more and more conscious, more and more luminous, more and more receptive, until it reaches a perfection sufficient for it to become a possible vehicle for the divine Force itself which will be able to use it as it uses the elements of the other parts of the creation, like the mind or the vital.

And at that moment the physical substance will be ready to manifest in the world the new Consciousness, new Light, new Will. Through all the centuries, through countless lives, passing through innumerable organisms, using countless experiences it, so to speak, becomes refined; it is prepared, and becomes more and more receptive and open to the divine Forces.

So, a man as a momentary individual being may not appear to progress. But the progress is continued through him, as through all organisms.[186]

The Psychic Being and Individual Progress

"This terrestrial evolutionary working of Nature from Matter to Mind and beyond it has a double process: there is an outward visible process of physical evolution with birth as its machinery, — for each evolved form of body housing its own evolved power of consciousness is maintained and kept in continuity by heredity; there is, at the same time, an invisible process of soul evolution with rebirth into ascending grades of form and consciousness as its machinery. The first by itself would mean only a cosmic evolution; for the individual would be a quickly perishing instrument, and the race, a more abiding collective

formulation, would be the real step in the progressive
manifestation of the cosmic Inhabitant, the universal Spirit:
rebirth is an indispensable condition for any long duration
and evolution of the individual being in the earth-exist-
ence. Each grade of cosmic manifestation, each type of
form that can house the indwelling Spirit, is turned by
rebirth into a means for the individual soul, the psychic
entity, to manifest more and more of its concealed consciousness; each life becomes a step in a victory over
Matter by a greater progression of consciousness in it
which shall make eventually Matter itself a means for the
full manifestation of the Spirit."

Sri Aurobindo, *The Life Divine*

It is difficult to understand, Sweet Mother.

Ah!...

If you take terrestrial history, all the forms of life have appeared one after another in a general plan, a general programme,
with the addition, always, of a new perfection and a greater
consciousness. Take just animal forms — for that is easier to
understand, they are the last before man — each animal that
appeared had an additional perfection in its general nature —
I don't mean in all the details — a greater perfection than the
preceding ones, and the crowning point of the ascending march
was the human form which, for the moment, from the point of
view of consciousness, is the form most capable of manifesting consciousness; that is, the human form at its height, at the
height of its possibilities, is capable of more consciousness
than all preceding animal forms.

This is *one* of Nature's ways of evolution.

Sri Aurobindo told us last week that this Nature was following an ascending progression in order to manifest more and more the divine consciousness contained in all forms. So, with each new form that it produces, Nature makes a form capable of expressing more completely the spirit which this form contains. But if it were like this, a form comes, develops, reaches its highest point and is followed by another form; the others do not disappear, but the individual does not progress. The individual dog or monkey, for instance, belongs to a species which has its own peculiar characteristics; when the monkey or the man arrives at the height of its possibilities, that is, when a human individual becomes the best type of humanity, it will be finished; the individual will not be able to progress any farther. He belongs to the human species, he will continue to belong to it. So, from the point of view of terrestrial history there is a progress, for each species represents a progress compared with the preceding species; but from the point of view of the individual, there is no progress: he is born, he follows his development, dies and disappears. Therefore, to ensure the progress of the individual, it was necessary to find another means; this one was not adequate. But within the individual, contained in each form, there is an organisation of consciousness which is closer to and more directly under the influence of the inner divine Presence, and the form which is under this influence — this kind of inner concentration of energy — has a life independent of the physical form — this is what we generally call the "soul" or the "psychic being" — and since it is organised around the divine centre it partakes of the divine nature which is immortal, eternal. The outer body falls away, and this remains throughout every experience that it has in each life, and there is a progress from life to life, and it is the progress of the *same* individual. And this movement complements the other, in the sense that instead of a species which progresses relative to other species, it is an individual who passes through all the stages of progress of these species and can continue to progress even when the species have reached the limit of their possibilities and... stay there or disappear — it depends on the case — but they cannot go any farther, whereas the individual, having a life independent of the purely material form, can pass from one form to another and continue his progress *indefinitely*. That makes a double movement which completes itself. And that is why each individual has the possibility of reaching the utmost realisation, independent of the form to which he momentarily belongs.

There are people — there used to be and there still are, I believe — who say they remember their past lives and recount what happened when they were dogs or elephants or monkeys, and tell you stories in great detail about what happened to them. I am not going to argue with them, but anyway this illustrates the fact that before being a man, one could have been a monkey — perhaps one doesn't have the power to remember it, that's another matter — but certainly, this inner divine spark has passed through successive forms in order to become more and more conscious of itself. And if it is proved that one can remember the form one had before becoming a psychic being as it is found in the human form, well, one might very well recollect climbing trees and eating coconuts and even playing all sorts of tricks on the traveller passing beneath!

In any case, the fact is there. Perhaps later we shall see that a certain state of inner organisation is necessary for this psychic being to be able to have memories in the way the mental being has them — we shall speak about it later, when we come to it in the book — but in any case the fact is established: it is this double movement of evolution intersecting and complementing itself which gives the utmost possibilities of realisation to the divine light within each being. This is what Sri Aurobindo has explained. (*Turning to the child*) This means that in your outer body you belong to the animal species in the course of becoming a supramental species — you are not that yet! but within you there's a psychic being which has already lived in many, many, countless species before and carries an experience of thousands of years within you, and which will continue while your human body remains human and finally decomposes.[187]

Progress from Life to Life

Mother, since in each new life the mind and vital as well as the body are new, how can the experiences of past lives be useful for them? Do we have to go through all the experiences once again?

That depends on people!

It is not the mind and vital which develop and progress

from life to life — except in altogether exceptional cases and at a very advanced stage of evolution — it is the psychic. So, this is what happens: the psychic has alternate periods of activity and rest; it has a life of progress resulting from experiences of the physical life, of active life in a physical body, with all the experiences of the body, the vital and the mind; then, normally, the psychic goes into a kind of rest for assimilation where the result of the progress accomplished during its active existence is worked out, and when this assimilation is finished, when it has absorbed the progress it had prepared in its active life on earth, it comes down again in a new body bringing with it the result of all its progress and, at an advanced stage, it even chooses the environment and the kind of body and the kind of life in which it will live to complete its experience concerning one point or another. In some very advanced cases the psychic can, before leaving the body, decide what kind of life it will have in its next incarnation.

When it has become an almost completely formed and already very conscious being, it presides over the formation of the new body, and usually through an inner influence it chooses the elements and the substance which will form its body in such a way that the body is adapted to the needs of its new experience. But this is at a rather advanced stage. And later, when it is fully formed and returns to earth with the idea of service, of collective help and participation in the divine Work, then it is able to bring to the body in formation certain elements of the mind and vital from previous lives which, having been organised and impregnated with psychic forces in previous lives, could be preserved and, consequently, can participate in the general progress. But this is at a very, very advanced stage.

When the psychic is fully developed and very conscious, when it becomes a conscious instrument of the divine Will, it organises the vital and the mind in such a way that they too participate in the general harmony and can be preserved.

A high degree of development allows at least some parts of the mental and vital beings to be preserved in spite of the dissolution of the body. If, for instance, some parts — mental or vital — of the human activity have been particularly developed, these elements of the mind and vital are maintained even "in their form" — in the form of the activity which has been fully organised — as, for example, in highly intellectual people who have particularly developed their brains, the mental part of their being keeps this structure and is preserved in the form of an organised brain which has its own life and can be kept unchanged until a future life so as to participate in it with all its gains.

In artists, as for instance in certain musicians who have used their hands in a particularly conscious way, the vital and mental substance is preserved in the form of hands, and these hands remain fully conscious, they can even use the body of living people if there is a special affinity — and so on.

Otherwise, in ordinary people in whom the psychic form is not fully developed and organised, when the psychic leaves the body, the mental and vital forms may persist for a certain time if the death has been particularly peaceful and concentrated, but if a man dies suddenly and in a state of passion, with numerous attachments, well, the different parts of the being are dispersed and live for a shorter or longer time their own life in their own domain, then disappear.

The centre of organisation and transformation is always the presence of the psychic in the body. Therefore, it is a very big mistake to believe that the progress continues or even, as some believe, that it is more complete and rapid in the periods of transition between two physical lives; in general, there is no progress at all, for the psychic enters into a state of rest and the other parts, after a more or less ephemeral life in their own domain, are dissolved.

Earthly life is the place for progress. It is here, on earth, that progress is possible, during the period of earthly existence. And it is the psychic which carries the progress over from one life to another, by organising its own evolution and development itself.[188]

*

Does a being carry his mental, vital and physical experiences from one life to another?

Each case is different. It all depends on the degree of the individual's development in his different parts and on how well these parts are organised around the psychic centre. The more organised the being, the more consciously lasting it becomes. We can say in a general way that each person brings into his present life the consequences of his previous lives, without, however, preserving the memory of these lives. Apart from a few very rare exceptions, only when you are united with your psychic being and become fully conscious of it do you obtain, at the same time, the memory of past lives, which the psychic preserves in its consciousness.

Otherwise, even in those who are most sensitive, these memories are fragmentary, uncertain and intermittent. Most often they are hardly recognisable and seem to be nothing more than undefinable impressions. And yet a person who knows how to see through apprearances will be able to perceive a kind of similarity in the sequence of events in his life.[189]

Survival of the Mental Personality and Immortality

"Immortality is not the survival of the mental personality after death, though that also is true, but the waking possession of the unborn and deathless Self of which body is only an instrument and a shadow."

Sri Aurobindo, *Thoughts and Aphorisms*

There are three statements here which have raised questions. First, "What is the mental personality?"

In each human being the body is animated by the vital being, and governed, or partially governed, by a mental being. This is a general rule, but the extent to which the mental being is formed and individualised varies greatly from one individual to the next. In the great mass of human beings the mind is something fluid which has no organisation of its own, and therefore it is not a personality. And as long as the mind is like that, fluid, unorganised, with no cohesive life of its own and without personality, it cannot survive. What made up the mental being dissolves in the mental region when the body, the substance which made up the body, dissolves in the physical substance.

But as soon as the mental being is formed, organised, individualised, and has become a personality, it does not depend, it no longer depends on the body for its existence, and it therefore survives the body. The earth's mental atmosphere is filled with beings, mental personalities which lead an entirely independent existence, even after the disappearance of the body; they can reincarnate in a new body when the soul, that is to say, the true Self, reincarnates, thus carrying with it the memory of its previous lives.

But this is not what Sri Aurobindo calls Immortality. Immortality is a life without beginning or end, without birth or death, which is altogether independent of the body. It is the life of the Self, the essential being of each individual, and it is not separate from the universal Self. And this essential being has a sense of oneness with the universal Self; it is in fact a personified, individualised expression of the universal Self and has neither beginning nor end, neither life nor death, it exists eternally and that is what is immortal. When we are fully conscious of this Self we participate in its eternal life, and we therefore become immortal.[190]

Discovery of the Soul

Every human being carries hidden within him the possibility of a greater consciousness which goes beyond the bounds of his present life and enables him to share in a higher and a vaster life. Indeed, in all exceptional beings it is always this consciousness that governs their lives and organises both the circumstances of their existence and their individual reaction to these circumstances. What the human mental consciousness does not know and cannot do, this consciousness knows and does. It is like a light that shines at the centre of the being, radiating through the thick coverings of the external consciousness. Some have a vague intimation of its presence; a good many children are under its influence, which shows itself very distinctly at times in their spontaneous actions and even in their words. Unfortunately, since parents most often do not know what it is and do not understand what is happening in their child, their reaction to these phenomena is not a good one and all their education consists in making the child as unconscious as possible in this domain and concentrating all his attention on external things, thus accustoming him to think that they are the only ones that matter. It is true that this concentration on external things is very useful, provided that it is done in the proper way. The three lines of education — physical, vital and mental — deal with that and could be defined as the means of building up the personality, raising the individual out of the amorphous subconscious mass and making him a well-defined self-conscious entity. With psychic education we come to the problem of the true motive of existence, the purpose of life on earth, the discovery to which this life must lead and the result of that discovery: the consecration of the individual to his eternal principle. Normally this discovery is associated with a mystic feeling, a religious life, because it is mainly the religions that have concerned themselves with this aspect of life. But it need not necessarily be so: the mystic notion of God may be replaced by the more philosophical notion of truth and still the discovery will remain essentially the same, but the road leading to it may be taken even by the most intransigent positivist. For mental notions and ideas have only a very secondary importance in preparing one for the psychic life. The important thing is to live the experience; that carries with it its own reality and force apart from any theory that may precede or accompany or follow it, for most often theories are no more than explanations that one gives to oneself in order to have, more or less, the illusion of knowledge. Man clothes the ideal or the absolute he seeks to attain with different names according to the environment in which he is born and the education he has received. The experience is essentially the same, if it is sincere; it is only the words and phrases in which it is formulated that differ according to the belief and the mental education of the one who has the experience. All formulation is thus only an approximation that should be progressive and grow in precision as the experience itself becomes more and more precise and co-ordinated. Still, to sketch a general outline of psychic education, we must give some idea, however relative it may be, of what we mean by the psychic being. One could say, for example, that the creation of an individual being is the result of the projection, in time and space, of one of the countless possibilities latent in the supreme origin of all manifestation which, through the medium of the one and universal consciousness, takes concrete form in the law or the truth of an individual and so, by a progressive development, becomes his soul or psychic being.

I must emphasise that what is stated briefly here does not claim to be a complete exposition of the reality and does not exhaust the subject — far from it. It is only a very summary explanation for a practical purpose, to serve as a basis for the education which we intend to consider now.

It is through this psychic presence that the truth of an individual being comes into contact with him and the circumstances of his life. In most cases the presence acts, so to say, from behind the veil, unrecognised and unknown; but in some, it is perceptible and its action recognisable and even, in a very few, the presence becomes tangible and its action fully effective. These go forward in life with an assurance and a certitude all their own; they are masters of their destiny. It is for the purpose of obtaining this mastery and becoming conscious of the psychic presence that psychic education should be practised. But for that there is need of a special factor, the personal will. For till now, the discovery of the psychic being and identification with it have not been among the recognised subjects of education, and although one can find in special treatises useful and practical hints on the subject, and although in exceptional cases one may have the good fortune of meeting someone who is capable of showing the way and giving the help that is needed to follow it, most often the attempt is left to one's own personal initiative. The discovery is a personal matter and a great determination, a strong will and an untiring perseverance are indispensable to reach the goal. Each one must, so to say, trace out his own path through his own difficulties. The goal is known to some extent, for most of those who have reached it have described it more or less clearly. But the supreme value of the discovery lies in its spontaneity, its ingenuousness, and that escapes all ordinary mental laws. And that is why anyone wanting to take up the adventure usually first seeks out some person who has successfully undertaken it and is able to sustain him and enlighten him on his way. Yet there are some solitary travellers and for them a few general indications may be useful.

The starting-point is to seek in yourself that which is independent of the body and the circumstances of life, which is not born of the mental formation that you have been given, the language you speak, the habits and customs of the environment in which you live, the country where you are born or the age to which you belong. You must find, in the depths of your being, that which carries in it a sense of universality, limitless expansion, unbroken continuity. Then you decentralise, extend and widen yourself; you begin to live in all things and in all beings; the barriers separating individuals from each other break down. You think in their thoughts, vibrate in their sensations, feel in their feelings, live in the life of all. What seemed inert suddenly becomes full of life, stones quicken, plants feel and will and suffer, animals speak in a language more or less inarticulate, but clear and expressive; everything is animated by a marvellous consciousness without time or limit. And this is only one aspect of the psychic realisation; there are others, many others. All help you to go beyond the barriers of your egoism, the walls of your external personality, the impotence of your reactions and the incapacity of your will.

But, as I have already said, the path to that realisation is long and difficult, strewn with snares and problems to be solved, which demand an unfailing determination. It is like the explorer's trek through virgin forest in quest of an unknown land, of some great discovery. The psychic being is also a great discovery which requires at least as much fortitude and endurance as the discovery of new continents. A few simple words of advice may be useful to one who has resolved to undertake it.

The first and perhaps the most important point is that the mind is incapable of judging spiritual things. All those who have written on this subject have said so; but very few are those who have put it into practice. And yet, in order to proceed on the path, it is absolutely indispensable to abstain from all mental opinion and reaction.

Give up all personal seeking for comfort, satisfaction, enjoyment or happiness. Be only a burning fire for progress, take whatever comes to you as an aid to your progress and immediately make whatever progress is required.

Try to take pleasure in all you do, but never do anything for the sake of pleasure.

Never get excited, nervous or agitated. Remain perfectly calm in the face of all circumstances. And yet be always alert to discover what progress you still have to make and lose no time in making it.

Never take physical happenings at their face value. They are always a clumsy attempt to express something else, the true thing which escapes our superficial understanding.

Never complain of the behaviour of anyone, unless you have the power to change in his nature what makes him act in this way; and if you have the power, change him instead of complaining.

Whatever you do, never forget the goal which you have set before you. There is nothing great or small once you have

set out on this great discovery; all things are equally important and can either hasten or delay its success. Thus before
you eat, concentrate a few seconds in the aspiration that the
food you are about to eat may bring your body the substance
it needs to serve as a solid basis for your effort towards the
great discovery, and give it the energy for persistence and
perseverance in the effort.

Before you go to sleep, concentrate a few seconds in the
aspiration that the sleep may restore your fatigued nerves,
bring calm and quietness to your brain so that on waking you
may, with renewed vigour, begin again your journey on the
path of the great discovery.

Before you act, concentrate in the will that your action
may help or at least in no way hinder your march forward
towards the great discovery.

When you speak, before the words come out of your
mouth, concentrate just long enough to check your words
and allow only those that are absolutely necessary to pass,
only those that are not in any way harmful to your progress
on the path of the great discovery.

To sum up, never forget the purpose and goal of your life.
The will for the great discovery should be always there above
you, above what you do and what you are, like a huge bird of
light dominating all the movements of your being.

Before the untiring persistence of your effort, an inner
door will suddenly open and you will emerge into a dazzling
splendour that will bring you the certitude of immortality,
the concrete experience that you have always lived and always shall live, that external forms alone perish and that these
forms are, in relation to what you are in reality, like clothes

that are thrown away when worn out. Then you will stand erect, freed from all chains, and instead of advancing laboriously under the weight of circumstances imposed upon you by Nature, which you had to endure and bear if you did not want to be crushed by them, you will be able to walk on, straight and firm, conscious of your destiny, master of your life.[191]

GLOSSARY OF NAMES AND TERMS

The Glossary includes Sanskrit terms, certain proper names and special terms found in Sri Aurobindo's writings. Explanations of philosophical and psychological terms have generally been given in Sri Aurobindo's own words.

the Adversary — anti-divine Force that is in revolt against the Divine, against the Truth and Light, and opposed to the yoga; *see also* **Asura**.

Ananda — bliss, delight, beatitude, spiritual ecstasy; the essential principle of delight: a self-delight which is the very nature of the transcendent and infinite existence.

annamaya puruṣa — the physical being.

antarātman — inner self; soul.

aparārdha — the lower half (of world existence); the lower hemisphere.
     A separation, acute in practice though unreal in essence, divides the total being of man, the microcosm, as it divides also the world-being, the macrocosm. Both have a higher and a lower hemisphere, the *parārdha* and *aparārdha* of the ancient wisdom. The higher hemisphere is the perfect and eternal reign of the Spirit; for there it manifests without cessation or diminution its infinities, deploys the unconcealed glories of its illimitable existence, its illimitable consciousness and knowledge, its illimitable force and power, its illimitable beatitude. The lower hemisphere belongs equally to the Spirit; but here it is veiled, closely, thickly, by its inferior self-expression of limiting mind, confining life and dividing body.

asat — Non-being; non-existence; something beyond the last term to which we can reduce our purest conception and our most abstract or subtle experience of actual being as we know or can conceive of it while in this universe. This Nothing is merely a something beyond positive conception.

Asura — the strong or mighty one, Titan; a hostile being or force of the vital mental plane, known in traditional Indian legends as the dark Titan or demon; *see also* Adversary.

Asuric — of the nature of the Asura.

Atman — Self; Spirit; the original and essential nature of Existence or Being.

Augustine, St. — (354-430), a great saint, bishop of Hippo and one of the four Latin fathers of the Christian Church.

Being — the Self; the sole and fundamental Reality or Truth of existence; all that exists is part of the one indivisible Being.

The One Being manifests itself on different planes or levels of consciousness, and in the individual being is constituted by different distinguishable parts of the indivisible Being.

The part of our nature of which we are normally conscious is our surface or outer being consisting of the body, the (surface) vital (related to life-energy and emotions, desires, passions, etc.), and the (surface) mind (having to do with cognition, intelligence, ideas, thought perceptions, etc.).

Behind this superficial consciousness there exists a far greater, deeper and more powerful consciousness in touch with the universal planes of Mind, Life and Matter. This hidden consciousness, referred to as our inner being, consists of the inner mental, the inner vital and the inner physical, with the psychic (the soul) as the innermost being which, as an aspect of the central being, supports all the different parts in the manifestation and which develops over the course of evolution an individuality which is called the psychic being.

The inner being is also sometimes referred to as the subliminal (being) or subliminal consciousness. It opens above to the Superconscient and below to the Subconscient and the Inconscient.

bhakti (**Bhakti**) — devotion; love for the Divine.

Buddhi — intelligence-will; understanding; intellect; reason; thinking mind; the discriminating principle, at once intelligence and will.

central being — the portion of the Divine which supports the individual being and survives from life to life; it has two forms: *jivātman*, which is above the manifestation in life, presiding over it, and the psychic being, which stands behind mind, life and body in the manifestation, supporting them and using them as its instruments.

Chaitya Purusha (*caitya puruṣa*) — psychic Person; the psychic being.

Chit — consciousness.

desire-soul — the surface soul which expresses itself in our cravings, impulses, feelings, emotions, ambitions, etc.; it is distinguished from the true soul in us — the psychic being.

Dharma — law; the deepest law of one's nature; the right law of individual and social life; literally, that which one lays hold of and which holds things together.

Divine, the — the Supreme Truth, the Supreme Being from whom all have come and in whom all are.

environmental consciousness (being) — part of the being that each person carries around him, outside his body, by which he is in touch with others and with the universal forces.

gradations between mind and Supermind — higher ranges of mind overtopping our normal mind and leading to Supermind; these succesive states, levels or graded powers of being are hidden in our own superconscious parts. In an ascending order the gradations of spiritualised mind are:

    Higher Mind: a luminous thought-mind whose instrumentation is through an elevated thought-power and comprehensive mental sight. In the Higher Mind one becomes constantly and closely aware of the Self, the One everywhere and knows and sees habitually with that awareness.

    Illumined Mind: a mind no longer of higher thought, but of spiritual light; here the clarity of the intelligence, its tranquil daylight, gives place or subordinates itself to an intense lustre, a splendour and illumination of the Spirit.

    Intuition: a power of consciousness nearer and more intimate than the above-mentioned gradations to the original knowlege by identity. What is thought-knowledge in the Higher Mind becomes illumination in the Illumined Mind and direct intimate vision in the Intuition. This true and authentic intuition must be distinguished from a power of the ordinary mental reason which is too easily confused with it, that power of involved reasoning that reaches its conclusion by a bound and does not need the ordinary steps of the logical mind.

Overmind: The Overmind is a delegate of the Supramental Consciousness, its delegate to the cosmic Ignorance. The Supramental is the total Truth-Consciousness; the Overmind draws down the truths separately and gives them a separate identity.

Guruvada — the doctrine that stresses the indispensability of the *guru* to the spiritual seeker.

Higher Mind — *see under* **gradations between mind and Supermind**.

the Ignorance — the consciousness of Multiplicity as distinguished from the Knowledge, the consciousness of Unity; a view of the reality based on separative or egoistic consciousness.

Illumined Mind — *see under* **gradations between mind and Supermind**.

the Inconscient (Inconscience) — the most involved state of the Superconscience; all powers of the Superconscience progressively evolve and emerge out of the Inconscient, the first emergence being Matter.

inner being — the inner mind, inner vital, inner physical with the psychic behind as the inmost; *see also* **the subliminal**.

Intuition — 1. Insight without conscious reasoning. 2. Plane of consciousness between Illumined Mind and Overmind. *See under* **gradations between mind and Supermind**.

Jivatman (Jiva) — the individual Self; the individualised self or spirit of the created being; the Spirit individualised and upholding the living being in its evolution from birth to birth. The full term is Jivatman — the Atman or eternal self of the living being (Jiva). The Jivatman in its essence does not change or evolve; it stands above the personal evolution; within the evolution itself it is represented by the evolving psychic being which supports all the rest of the nature.

life-nature (the life) — *see* **the Vital**.

manomaya puruṣa (**Manomaya Purusha**) — mental Person, the mental being.

mechanical mind — a part of the mind closely connected with the physical mind; its nature is to go on repeating without use whatever has happened — recent events, impressions, old habitual thoughts or ways of thinking and feeling.

mind (the mental) — "mind" and "mental" connote specially that part of the nature which has to do with cognition and intelligence, with ideas, with mental or thought perceptions, the reactions of thought to things, with the truly mental movements and formations, mental vision and will, etc. that are part of man's intelligence. The ordinary mind has three main parts: mind proper, vital mind, and physical mind.

The **mind proper** is divided into three parts: the thinking mind or intellect, concerned with ideas and knowledge in their own right; the dynamic mind, concerned with the putting out of mental forces for the realisation of the ideas; and the externalising mind, concerned with the expression of ideas in life.

The **vital mind** or desire mind is a mind of dynamic will, action, desire; it is occupied with force and achievement and satisfaction and possession, with enjoyment and suffering, giving and taking, growth and expansion, etc.

The **physical mind** is that part of the mind which is concerned with physical things only; limited by the physical view and experience of things, it mentalises the experience brought by the contact of outward life and things, but does not go beyond that. The mechanical mind, closely connected with the physical mind, goes on repeating without use whatever has happened.

Overtopping the ordinary mind, hidden in our own superconscient parts, there are higher ranges of Mind, gradations of spiritualised mind leading to the Supermind. In ascending order they are: Higher

Mind, Illumined Mind, Intuition and Overmind. *See* **gradations between mind and supermind**.

Nature, Nature Force — the outer or executive side of the Conscious Force which forms and moves the worlds. The higher, divine Nature (Para Prakriti) is free from Ignorance and its consequences; the lower Nature (Apara Prakriti) is a mechanism of active Force put forth for the working of the evolutionary Ignorance. The lower nature of an individual—mind, life and body—are part of Prakriti.

Nirvana — extinction (not necessarily of all being, but of being as we know it, extinction of ego, desire and egoistic action and mentality).

outer (surface) being (self) — *See under* **Being**.

Overmind — *see under* **gradations between mind and Supermind**.

Paramatma — the supreme Self or Spirit, the Absolute.

parārdha — *See* **aparārdha**.

Prakriti — Nature; Nature-Force. "Existence is composed of Prakriti and Purusha, the consciousness that sees and the consciousness that executes and formalises what we see. The one we call Soul, the other Nature." (Sri Aurobindo); *see also* Purusha.

prāṇamaya puruṣa — soul in life; the (true) vital being.

the physical (being) — not the body alone, but the whole physical mind, vital, material nature.

physical mind — *See under* **mind**.

physical vital — the part of the vital that is turned entirely upon physical things, full of desires and greeds and seekings for pleasure on the physical plane.

psyche — the soul; spark of the Divine before it has evolved into an individualised being; the divine essence in the individual. In the course of the evolution, the soul grows and evolves in the form of a soul-personality, the psychic being. *See also* **psychic being** *and* **soul**.

the psychic — psychic being, the term is sometimes used for the psyche or soul. *See also* **psyche** *and* **psychic being**.

psychic being — the divine portion in the individual which evolves from life to life, growing, by its experiences until it becomes a fully conscious being. The term "soul" is often used as a synonym for "psychic being", but strictly speaking, the soul is the undifferentiated psychic essence, whereas the psychic being is the individualised soul-personality developed by the psychic essence in the course of evolution. *See also* **the psychic**, *soul*, *and* **soul-personality**.

Purusha — Conscious Being; Conscious-Soul; essential being supporting the play of Prakriti; the Purusha represents the true being on whatever plane it manifests — physical, vital, mental, psychic.

Rig-veda — the Veda of the Riks (words of illumination), the most ancient of the sacred books of India.

Russell, Bertrand — (1872-1970), English philosopher.

Sachchidananda (Sat-Chit-Ananda) — the One Divine Being with a triple aspect of Existence (Sat), Consciousness (Chit) and Delight (Ananda). God is Sachchidananda; He manifests Himself as infinite Existence of which the essentiality is Consciousness, of which again the essentiality is bliss, is self-delight.

Sadhana — the practice of yoga.

Samadhi — yogic trance (in which the mind acquires the capacity of withdrawing from its limited waking activities into freer and higher states of consciousness).

Sanskara — association, impression, fixed notion, habitual reaction formed by one's past.

the Self — the Atman, the universal Spirit, the self-existent Being, the conscious essential Existence, one in all. The Self is being, not a being; it is the original and essential nature of our existence.

soul — the psychic essence or entity, the divine essence in the individual; a spark of the Divine that comes down into the manifestation to support the evolution of the individual. In the course of the evolution, the soul grows and evolves in the form of a soul-personality, the psychic being. The term "soul" is also often used as a synonym for "psychic being". *See also* **the psychic** *and* **psychic being**.

soul-personality —the psychic being or soul-form developing through evolution and passing from life to life. *See* **psychic being**.

Spirit — the Consciousness above mind, the Atman or universal Self which is always in oneness with the Divine.

spark-soul — *see* **psyche**.

the subconscient — the subconscient or subconscious of the individual is that submerged part of his being in which there is no waking conscious and coherent thought, will, feeling or organised reaction, but which yet receives obscurely the impressions of all things and stores them up; from it too all sorts of stimuli, of persistent habitual movements can surge up into dream or into the waking state. In the ordinary man the subconscient includes the larger part of the vital being and the physical mind and the secret body-consciousness. It is not to be confused with the subliminal: the subconscient is a *nether* diminished consciousness, the subliminal is an *inner* consciousness larger than our surface existence.

the subliminal — the inner being, taken in its entirety of inner mind, inner life, inner physical, with the soul or psychic entity supporting them. The subliminal in man is the largest part of his nature; it is not subconscient, but conscient and greater than the waking consciousness. The subconscient is that which is *below* the ordinary physical consciousness, the subliminal that which is *behind* and supports it.

Supermind — the Supramental, the Truth-Consciousness, the Divine Gnosis, the highest divine consciousness and force operative in the universe. A principle of consciousness superior to mentality, it exists, acts and proceeds in the fundamental truth and unity of things and not like the mind in their appearances and phenomenal divisions. Its fundamental character is knowledge by identity, by which the Self is known, the Divine Sachchidananda is known, but also the truth of manifestation is known because this too is that.

tamas (**Tamas**) — the quality that hides or darkens; the quality of ignorance, inertia and obscurity, of incapacity and inaction; the force of inconscience. Tamas is one of the three Gunas or modes of Nature.

Upanishads — a class of Hindu sacred writings, regarded as the source of the Vedanta philosophy.

vairāgya — distaste, disgust for the world and life.

the vital (being) — the life-nature made up of desires, sensations, feelings, passions, energies of action and of all the play of possessive and other related instincts, such as anger, fear, greed, lust, etc. The vital has three main parts:

higher vital: the mental vital and emotional vital taken together. The mental vital gives a mental expression by thought, speech or otherwise to the emotions, desires, passions, sensations or other movements of the vital being; the emotional vital is the seat of various feelings, such as love, joy, sorrow, hatred and the rest.

central vital or **vital proper**: dynamic, sensational and passionate, it is the seat of the stronger vital longings and reactions, such as ambition, pride, fear, love of fame, attractions and repulsions, desires and passions of various kinds and the field of many vital energies.

lower vital: made up of the smaller movements of human life-desire and life-reactions, it is occupied with small desires and feelings, such as food desire, sexual desire, small likings, dislikings, vanity, quarrels, love of praise, anger at blame, little wishes of all kinds, etc.

vital mind — a sort of mediator between the vital and the mental proper; a part of the nature of the mind whose function is not to think and reason, to perceive, consider and find out or value things, but to plan or dream or imagine what can be done; *see also under* **mind**.

vital-physical — the nervous part of the being; the life-force closely enmeshed in the reactions, desires, needs, sensations of the body.

Yoga — the discipline by which one seeks consciously and deliberately to realise union with the Divine or, more generally, to attain a higher consciousness.

REFERENCES

Passages in this book, serially numbered 1-191, have been extracted from the following volumes of the Sri Aurobindo Birth Centenary Library (1970-1973) and the Collected Works of the Mother (1972-87) published by Sri Aurobindo Ashram, Pondicherry.

Sri Aurobindo Birth Centenary Library (SABCL)

Vol.	Title
15	*Social and Political Thought*
19	*The Life Divine — Book Two Part Two*
20	*The Synthesis of Yoga — Parts One and Two*
21	*The Synthesis of Yoga — Parts Three and Four*
22	*Letters on Yoga — Part One*
23	*Letters on Yoga — Parts Two and Three*
24	*Letters on Yoga — Part Four*

Collected Works of the Mother (CWM)

Vol.	Title
3	*Questions and Answers*
4	*Questions and Answers 1950-51*
5	*Questions and Answers 1953*
6	*Questions and Answers 1954*
7	*Questions and Answers 1955*
8	*Questions and Answers 1956*
9	*Questions and Answers 1957-58*
10	*On Thoughts and Aphorisms*
12	*On Education*
14	*Words of the Mother*
15	*Words of the Mother*
16	*Some Answers from the Mother*
17	*More Answers from the Mother*

References are given below in an abbreviated form. The initial numeral is the serial number of the passage in this book located at the end of each passage. This is followed by the abbreviated title of the series (SABCL or CWM), followed by the volume number and the page number(s) where the passage occurs. For example:

1. SABCL: 15:37 indicates that passage 1 is to be found in the Sri Aurobindo Birth Centenary Library, Volume 15, p. 37.

Our Manifold Being

1. SABCL 15:37
2. CWM 7:42-43
3. CWM 7:215-16
4. SABCL 22:233
5. SABCL 22:303
6. SABCL 22:303
7. CWM 3:127
8. CWM 15:309
9. CWM 5:8-9
10. SABCL 20:68-69
11. SABCL 20:435

Planes and Parts of the Being

12. SABCL 20:429
13. SABCL 21:604
14. SABCL 24:1499-1500
15. SABCL 20:371-72
16. SABCL 22:347
17. SABCL 22:351
18. SABCL 22:352
19. SABCL 22:352
20. SABCL 22: 348
21. CWM 4:63
22. SABCL 24:1564
23. SABCL 24:1565
24. SABCL 24:1565
25. CWM 4:272-74
26. SABCL 22:347
27. SABCL 24:323-24
28. CWM 15:315-16
29. CWM 6:139-40
30. CWM 8:300-01
31. SABCL 22:323
32. CWM 8:304
33. CWM 6:355-56
34. CWM 12:55-56
35. SABCL 24:1297
36. SABCL 24:1297
37. CWM 5:257-59
38. CWM 7:37
39. CWM 8:298-99
40. SABCL 22:344-45
41. SABCL 22:320-21
42. CWM 6:306-08
43. CWM 8:190
44. CWM 7:170-72
45. CWM 10:14-16
46. SABCL 22:334-35
47. SABCL 22:341
48. SABCL 22:327
49. SABCL 22:347-48
50. CWM 14:366
51. CWM 6:318-19

52. SABCL 22:329
53. CWM 6:319-21
54. CWM 7:143-44
55. SABCL 22:353
56. SABCL 22:354-55
57. SABCL 22:360
58. SABCL 24:1597
59. CWM 14:389
60. SABCL 24:1712-13
61. SABCL 22:9
62. CWM 4:240
63. CWM 15:316-17
64. CWM 15:317-18
65. SABCL 22:348-50
66. SABCL 23:1020-21
67. SABCL 24:1606
68. CWM 7:108-09
69. CWM 7:109-112
70. SABCL 22:360
71. SABCL 22:313
72. SABCL 22:313-14
73. SABCL 24:1601-02
74. SABCL 24:1712-13
75. SABCL 24:1597
76. SABCL 22:308
77. SABCL 24:1159
78. SABCL 19:932-33
79. SABCL 19:938
80. SABCL 9:342
81. SABCL 19:944
82. SABCL 21:783-84
83. SABCL 23:1057-58
84. CWM 3:173-74
85. CWM 6:415-17
86. SABCL 24:1195
87. SABCL 24:1195
88. SABCL 22:299
89. SABCL 22:286
90. SABCL 22:267
91. SABCL 22:265
92. SABCL 22:270
93. SABCL 22:270
94. SABCL 22:274
95. SABCL 22:267
96. SABCL 22:282-83
97. SABCL 22:267-68
98. CWM 4:140-41
99. SABCL 22:268-69
100. SABCL 22:288-89
101. CWM 4:137
102. SABCL 22:295-96
103. CWM 7:221-22
104. SABCL 22:293-94
105. CWM 7:42
106. SABCL 22:300
107. CWM 7:263-64
108. CWM 7:253
109. CWM 14:351
110. CWM 6:160-61
111. CWM 6:447-48
112. CWM 6:334
113. SABCL 24:1097-98
114. CWM 7:272-73
115. SABCL 22:277-78
116. SABCL 22:279
117. SABCL 22:300
118. SABCL 22:309

Becoming an Individual

119. CWM 6:333-34

120. CWM 6:334-36
121. CWM 7:11-12
122. CWM 6:256-59
123. CWM 6:260-61
124. CWM 7:365-66

Becoming Conscious

125. SABCL 24:1558
126. CWM 4:33-37
127. CWM 3:1-2
128. SABCL 24:1607
129. CWM 12:3-4
130. CWM 4:360-62
131. SABCL 24:1694-95
132. CWM 12:21-22
133. SABCL 24:1297-98
134. CWM 4:244
135. SABCL 24:1398
136. CWM 4:68-69
137. CWM 5:31
138. CWM 8:368-69

Organisation, Harmonisation Unification

139. CWM 14:355
140. CWM 17:156
141. CWM 14:354
142. CWM 15:310
143. CWM 16:410
144. CWM 7:1-2
145. CWM 16:362-63
146. SABCL 19:897-98
147. CWM 16:396
148. CWM 3:7
149. CWM 5:9-11

150. CWM 7:295-96
151. CWM 4:80-81
152. CWM 8:174-76
153. SABCL 22: 52-54
154. CWM 16:432

Some Answers and Explanations

155. CWM 12:77-79
156. CWM 6:1
157. CWM 4:260-62
158. CWM 9:43-48
159. CWM 7: 256-57
160. CWM 10:87-88
161. CWM 7:253-55
162. CWM 8:280-81
163. CWM 6:16-17
164. CWM 6:421-23
165. CWM 6:426
166. CWM 6:427-28
167. CWM 4: 40-42
168. CWM 6:428-29
169. CWM 8: 380-81
170. CWM 7: 371-372
171. CWM 9:308-11
172. CWM 10:23-26
173. CWM 9:357-60
174. CWM 8:284-86
175. CWM 8: 282-83
176. CWM 10:54-55
177. CWM 16:368-69
178. CWM 6:346-48
179. CWM 9:327-29
180. CWM 10:80-82
181. CWM 4:38-40
182. CWM 8:191-92

183. CWM 4:228-229
184. CWM 4: 164-65
185. CWM 7: 422-424
186. CWM 7: 425-427
187. CWM 9:213-16

188. CWM 9:268-70
189. CWM 10: 97
190. CWM 10:27-28
191. CWM 12:30-35

INDEX

Other Titles by Sri Aurobindo & The Mother

Compiled by Dr. A.S. Dalal

Psychic Being (Soul: Its Nature, Mission, Evolution)
by Sri Aurobindo & The Mother

The present compilation is an attempt to bring together in one volume the manifold teachings pertaining to the psychic being which are to be found in the numerous works of Sri Aurobindo and The Mother. The selections deal with the nature of the psychic being, shedding the light of Sri Aurobindo and The Mother on the inner constitution of the human being and on various related questions such as the process of inner growth, the afterlife, and rebirth.

Trade Paper   ISBN 0-941524-56-6   223 pp pb $8.95

Living Words
by Sri Aurobindo & The Mother

Inspiring selections from the works of Sri Aurobindo and the Mother dealing with spiritual growth towards a new consciousness beyond mind which has now manifested itself upon the earth, heralding the birth of a New World.

Trade Paper   198 pp pb   ISBN 0-910261-42-3 $5.95

Hidden Forces of Life
by Sri Aurobindo & The Mother

Dealt with herein are the diverse forces which act on us, determining the course of events, influencing our thoughts, feelings and actions, affecting our moods, health and level of energy, pulling the human being to nether depths or beckoning him towards lofty heights. Also shown are the hidden forces behind evolution and the universal action.

Trade Paper   203 pp pb   ISBN 0-941524-60-4 $9.95

Available at bookstores and natural food stores nationwide or order your copy directly by sending cost of book(s) plus $2.50 shipping/handling ($.75 s/h for each additional copy ordered at the same time) to:

Lotus Press, PO Box 325, Twin Lakes, WI 53181 USA
toll free order line: 800 824 6396   office phone: 262 889 8561
office fax: 262 889 2461 lotuspress@lotuspress.com www.lotuspress.com

Lotus Press is the publisher of a wide range of books and software in the field of alternative health and spirituality, including Sri Aurobindo's writings, Ayurveda, Chinese medicine, Reiki and energetic healing modalities. Request our free book catalog.